This is the page where we usually have the copyright stuff like:

But since I want to lead by example, I will allow you to create an improved copy of this book and use it for a non-commercial use, without being scared that I will sue you. I won't. Here's the proof:

This book would not have been possible without the support of the believers who have given through my crowdfunding campaign on Kickstarter. Cheers to them, 5 000 times.

Eric Lafontaine

Walid Khoder

Mark Baker

Michael Rousseau

Louise Hebert

Danielle Hébert

Eliane Gamache

Benoit Sansoucy

Vladimir Evdokimov

Jennifer Young

Marc-André Riendeau

Hugo Archambault

Marc-Andre Tremblay

Louis-Philippe Dea

Marc-Andre Charette

Simon Labrecque

Robin Quenneville

Catherine

Louis-Charles Primeau

Joelle Desaulniers

Sébastien Levert

Helene

Kym Archambault

Laurence St-Aubin

Lawrence Hébert

Stephanie V. Peters

Eyal Arel

Scott Gillespie

Dominique Bourgoin

Leclerc Richard

Josh Swank

Pascal Fafard

Antoine Bonicalzi

Dominic Pinto

Jocelyne Leblanc

Caroline Roussel

Cloud Richer

Valerie Messier

Melanie Dulong

Louis Michel Gratton

Gabriel Varin

Joe Player

Ian Savoie

Alexandre Quenneville

Chantal Bossé

Pierre

Pascal Veilleux
Marc-Alexandre Labrecque
David Leroux
Laurie Millette
Stephane Pelletier
Mathieu Champagne
Lisa Temes
Francois-Pierre Marcil
Jennifer Morin
Catherine
Marc-Olivier Vincent
Dominic Lanteigne
Christian Laventure
Pete Archambault
Carl Gourgue
Zachary Fleischmann
Louiis Paskall
F.L.
Michael Morin
Fernanda Pacheco
Carolane Tremblay
Krysten
Deepra Smith
Kevin Trieu
Alan Jones
Jessica Allard
Anthony Battah
Ugo Schraenen
Vincent
Insurgent Publishing
MakerBloks
Sylvie Coulombe
Stephanie Pare
Martin Wiedenhoff
Nicolas Blanchard

Erik Bolamba
Sloane|BAXTER
David Sigouin
Guillaume Savard
Richard Ng-Jobidon
Audrey Ravoux
Mauro Sicard
Chantal Gougeon
Muiz Manan
Glen Bodor
Earendil Engelmann
Adrian van Wijk
Anne Malouin
Cubergreen
Marie France Binette
Chantal Paquin
Caroline Plourde
Sophie Harvey
Valérie Chouinard-Audette
Jason
Gabriel Voicu
Michaël St-Jean
Jimmy
Simon Robert
Jean-Philippe Albert
Chris Herbert
Simon Raharinaivo
Christiane Theoret
William
Sarah Thompson
Chad Ryg
Michelle Roy

You see, a book, like any business, will evolve to become better, or die.

Throughout this story, I invite you to write down your experiences at the end of each chapter or simply submit them online at http://bit.ly/shortcutstosuccessandhappiness.

I'll do the same. The best stories will appear in the next version of this book.

There are two schools of thought.

The most dominant says that we need to reach success before we can even dream of reaching happiness. This school of thought follows this math:

Success = Happiness

The other school of thought—smaller, but rising—dares to say we have to find happiness before we can really be successful. Its proponents contend we need to flip the previous equation on its head:

Happiness = Success

I sit between both of these positions. I believe there is a path to finding both success and happiness at the same time. For me, rather than one being predicated on the other, they are commingled, and they should not be considered as the destination, but as life's journey.

success

But maybe I'm just a fool...

- *I'm tired of this life.*

Here is a typical statement of one whose head is about to explode. Have you ever felt this way? I did.

Were you, like many young corporate employees, promised to a great career, but deep inside, you felt you were meant to be an entrepreneur? I was.

I was a few seconds away from puking my whole life.

I felt like a prisoner within a prison that I myself had put a great amount of effort and sweat into building.

Actually, I felt as if my life looked like random and angry keyboard strokes: *!?#*@(**%!#*\.

Then, out of nowhere, a friend of mine, in a stroke of insight, suggested I reboot my whole system. He said:

- Man, come on! Reboot your crappy mental computer. Press:

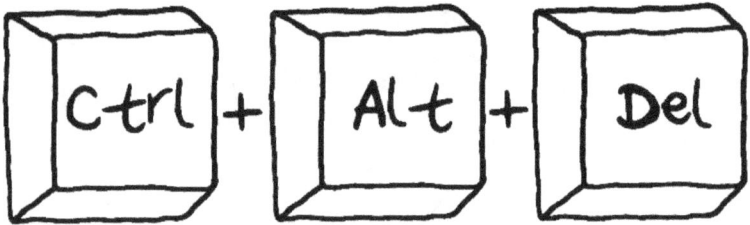

Ctrl + Alt + Del

And he gave me this book.

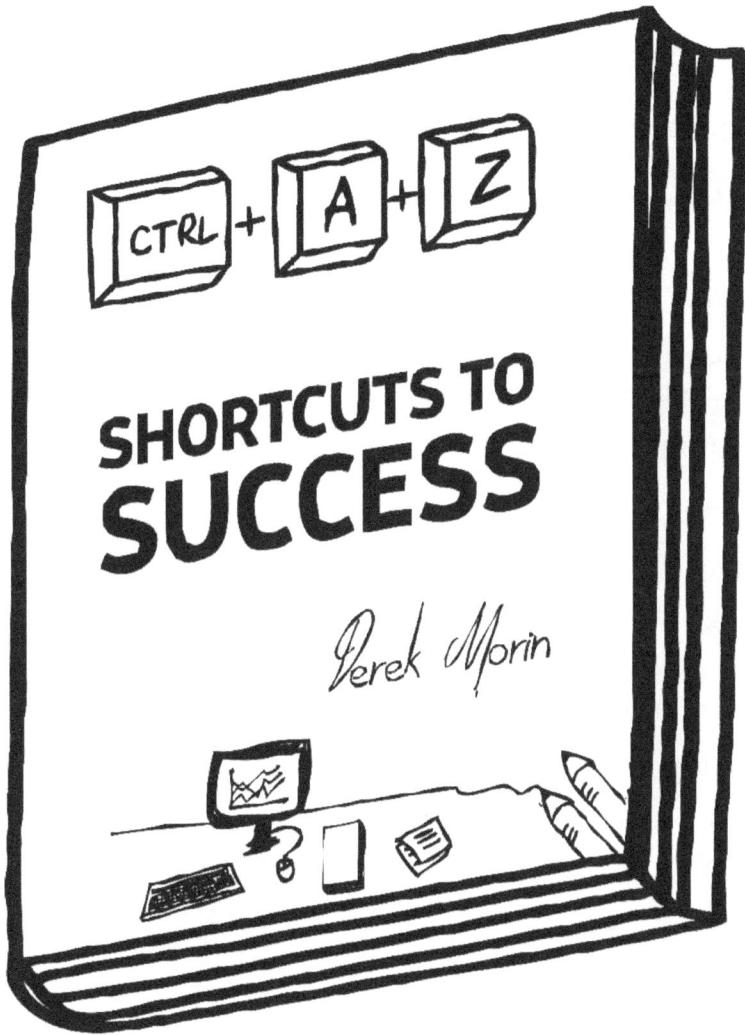

I opened it.

Contents

ENTREPRENEUR

So, you want to become an entrepreneur. Why?

a) You are doing a job you don't like.
b) You hate your boss.
c) You want to get rich.
d) You idolized Steve Jobs.
e) You want to retire at 40.
f) You want to be free to do what you want, when you want.
g) All of the above.
h) None of the above.

You answered G, right?

However, you probably have no idea what being an entrepreneur implies or where to start.

The following shortcuts propose you start from who you are to create a company that looks like you: great and unique.

But... who are you?

P.S. If you answered H, close this book. You're wasting your time, unless you're really curious and want to know who you are.

Ctrl-A: Select all

Life is a circle. Only you can make it vicious.

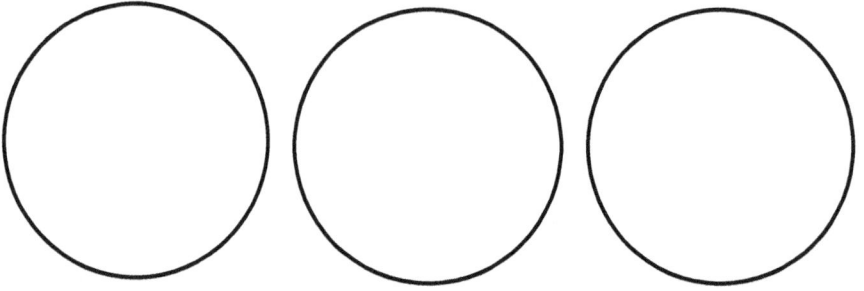

Once upon a time, there were three circles.

These three circles represent the overall picture of your life—the *Big Picture*, as we say in English. We will refer to this as the big PIC.

Let's take a closer look.

Personality circle

Inside the first circle is your personality.

Summarize your strengths in just three words. Choose words that evoke your qualities. Let me guess: you don't have a clue, do you?

On the next page, there is a list of 100 adjectives you can use to positively describe your personality.

100 adjectives
to positively describe someone's personality

Agreeable	Discreet	Hilarious	Responsible
Alert	Dynamic	Impartial	Seemly
Alluring	Eager	Instinctive	Selective
Ambitious	Easy-going	Joyous	Self-assured
Amused	Efficient	Kind	Sensitive
Boundless	Enchanting	Kind-hearted	Shrewd
Bright	Encouraging	Knowledgeable	Sincere
Calm	Energetic	Likeable	Skillful
Capable	Entertaining	Lively	Smiling
Charming	Enthusiastic	Lovely	Steadfast
Cheerful	Excited	Loving	Stimulating
Coherent	Fair	Lucky	Successful
Comfortable	Faithful	Mature	Succinct
Confident	Fantastic	Obedient	Talented
Cooperative	Fearless	Pains-taking	Thoughtful
Courageous	Frank	Peaceful	Thrifty
Credible	Friendly	Pleasant	Trustworthy
Cultured	Funny	Productive	Unbiased
Dashing	Generous	Protective	Unusual
Debonair	Gentle	Proud	Upbeat
Decisive	Glorious	Punctual	Vigorous
Decorous	Good	Receptive	Vivacious
Detailed	Happy	Reliable	Willing
Determined	Harmonious	Resolute	Wise
Diligent	Helpful	Resourceful	Witty

The personality circle is deliberately small to ensure that only the essential penetrates.

So go ahead and insert three words or less inside the circle. Difficult, isn't it? That's normal. Most people—especially those who, ironically, find it easy to talk about others—are unable to describe themselves, let alone in three words!

Because others usually know us better than we know ourselves, call someone who is close to you and who is especially honest: your spouse, a parent, a friend, a colleague. Ask him or her to describe your personality in three words. Then repeat the exercise with at least two other people.

	Contact 1	Contact 2	Contact 3
Word 1			
Word 2			
Word 3			

If you ask more people, the key is to identify the similarities to validate the strengths of your personality. Do the following:

1) Eliminate the unique words that occur only once.
2) Keep the answers that come back more than once.
3) Say these words aloud. Do they resonate with you? Do they strike any feelings within you? How intense? Why?

Finally, inside your personality circle, insert the words that describe who you are.

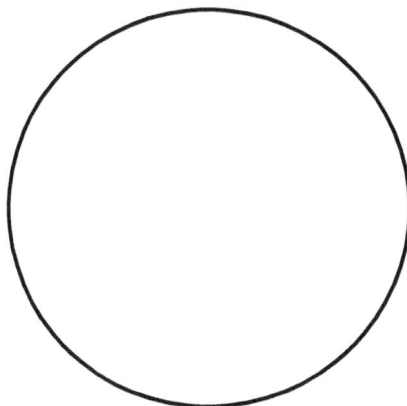

Interests circle

Inside the second circle are your interests.

What are they? In other words, what are the three things you care about most?

To help you, on the next page there is a list of 100 interests.

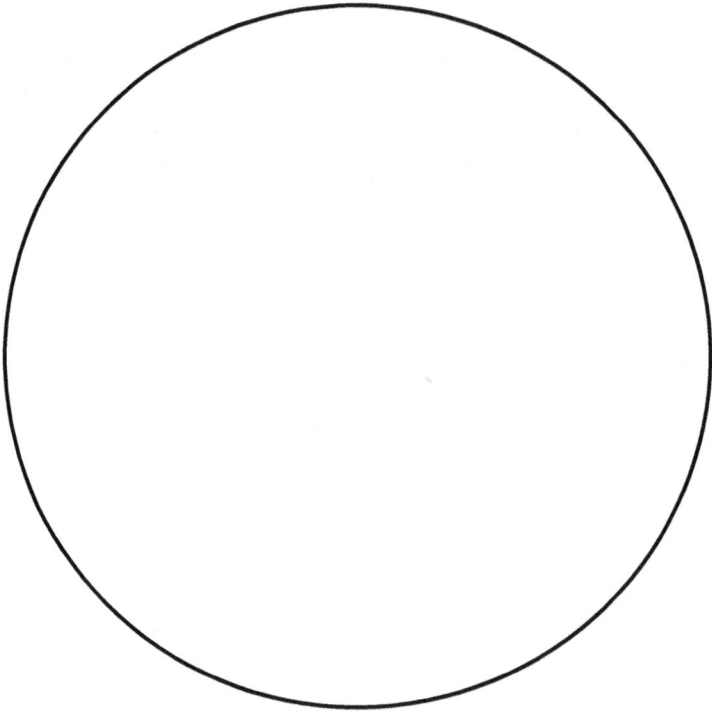

100 interests[1]

3D printing	Digital arts	Hunting	Photography
Acting	Dowsing	Ice skating	Playing musical
Air sports	Drama	Inline skating	Pottery
Amateur radio	Drawing	Instruments	Puzzles
Archery	Driving	Jewelry making	Quilting
Astronomy	Electronics	Jigsaw puzzles	Reading
Base jumping	Embroidery	Jogging	Scrapbooking
Baton twirling	Fishing	Juggling	Sculpting
Bird watching	Fitness	Kabaddi	Sewing
Blacksmithing	Flag football	Kayaking	Singing
Board games	Flower arranging	Kite flying	Sketching
Board sports	Flying	Knapping	Soapmaking
Bodybuilding	Foraging	Knife making	Sports
Brazilian Jiu-Jitsu	Gambling	Knitting	Stand-up comedy
Calligraphy	Gaming	Lacemaking	Sudoku
Candle making	Gardening	Lapidary	Table tennis
Coloring	Genealogy	Leather crafting	Taxidermy
Cooking	Geocaching	Lego building	Theater
Cosplaying	Ghost hunting	Listening to music	Video gaming
Couponing	Graffiti	Machining	Watching movies
Creative writing	Gunsmithing	Macrame	Web surfing
Crocheting	Handball	Magic	Woodworking
Cryptography	Hiking	Model building	Worldbuilding
Cycling	Homebrewing	Origami	Writing
Dance	Hooping	Painting	Yoga

Apply the same validation process as you did for the first circle. Call your friends and ask them to tell you what your interests are.

	Contact 1	Contact 2	Contact 3
Interest 1			
Interest 2			
Interest 3			

---

[1] Source: https://en.wikipedia.org/wiki/List_of_hobbies

Competencies circle

Finally, within the third circle are your competencies.

Enter below your top three skills, whether innate or acquired. What do you do with ease compared to others?

To help you, on the next pages there appears non-exhaustive lists of soft and hard skills.

Soft Skills[2]
Subjective interpersonal skills that are hard to quantify

Acceptation of criticism	Diversity awareness	Management	Research
Acceptation of feedback	Effective communication	Managing hard talks	Resilience
Adaptability	Emotional intelligence	Managing remote teams	Respectful
Artistic sense	Empathy	Meeting management	Results oriented
Assertiveness	Enthusiasm	Mentoring	Safety consciousness
Body language	Entrepreneurial thinking	Motivating	Scheduling
Business etiquette	Ergonomic sensitivity	Multi-tasking	Self awareness
Business trend awareness	Facilitation	Negotiation	Self confidence
Coaching	Flexibility	Networking	Self management
Collaboration	Focus	Office politics	Storytelling
Commitment	Friendliness	Organization	Strategic planning
Competitiveness	Giving feedback	Patience	Stress management
Conflict resolution	Honesty	Performance management	Supervision
Crisis management	Humor	Perseverance/persistence	Talent management
Critical observation	Independence	Personal branding	Team building
Critical thinking	Influence/persuasion	Persuasion	Team player
Deal making	Innovation	Planning	Technology savvy
Dealing with people	Inspiring	Positive work ethic	Thinking outside the box
Decision making	Intercultural competence	Presentation skills	Time management
Dedication	Interpersonal relationships	Problem solving	Tolerance of change
Delegation	Interviewing	Process improvement	Training
Design sense	Knowledge management	Public speaking	Verbal communication
Desire to learn	Leadership	Punctuality	Visual communication
Diplomacy	Listening	Quick-wittedness	Work-life balance
Dispute resolution	Making deadlines	Reliable	Writing

[2] Sources : http://training.simplicable.com/training/new/87-soft-skills and http://jobsearch.about.com/od/skills/fl/soft-skills.htm

Hard Skills
Teachable abilities (including some jobs) that are easy to quantify

A degree or certificate	Dentist	Market research analyst	Presentation specialist
Accounting	Dictation	Marketing	Product designer
Actuary	Driving online traffic	Mathematics	Programming
Administrative/Secretarial	Ecologist	Mechanic	Project management
Advertising	Economist	Media planner/buyer	Proofreading/editing
Agriculturist	Electrician	Mentoring staff	Psychologist
Air traffic controller	Engineer	Meteorologist	Public administrator
Aircraft pilot	Event management	Midwife	Real estate
Architect	Finance	Military officer	Sales
Astronomer	Firefighter	Networking	Scientist
Awareness of the law	Foreign language	Nursing	Sea captain
Banking	Geneticist	Occupational therapist	Social bookmarking
Biologist	Geologist	Oceanographer	Social media
Bookkeeping	Graphic design	Office manager	Social worker
Botanist	Human resources	Operation of machinery	Statistician
Business analyst	Immunologist	Optometrist	Surgeon
Cashier	Information technology	Painting	Surveyor
Chemist	Insurance	Pathologist	Teacher
Chiropractor	Interpreter	Personal assistant	Technical language
Claims adjuster	Journalism	Pharmacist	Trainer
Clergy	Judge	Pharmacologist	Typing/Audio typing
Consulting	Lawyer	Philosopher	Urban planner
Copywriting	Legal	Physical therapist	Veterinarian
Customer service	Librarian	Physician	Virologist
Database software	Link building	Police officer	Word/Spreadsheets

Apply the same validation process as you did for the first two circles. Call your friends and ask them to tell you what your competencies are.

	Contact 1	Contact 2	Contact 3
Competency 1			
Competency 2			
Competency 3			

Have you succeeded? If so, here is your life's big PIC.

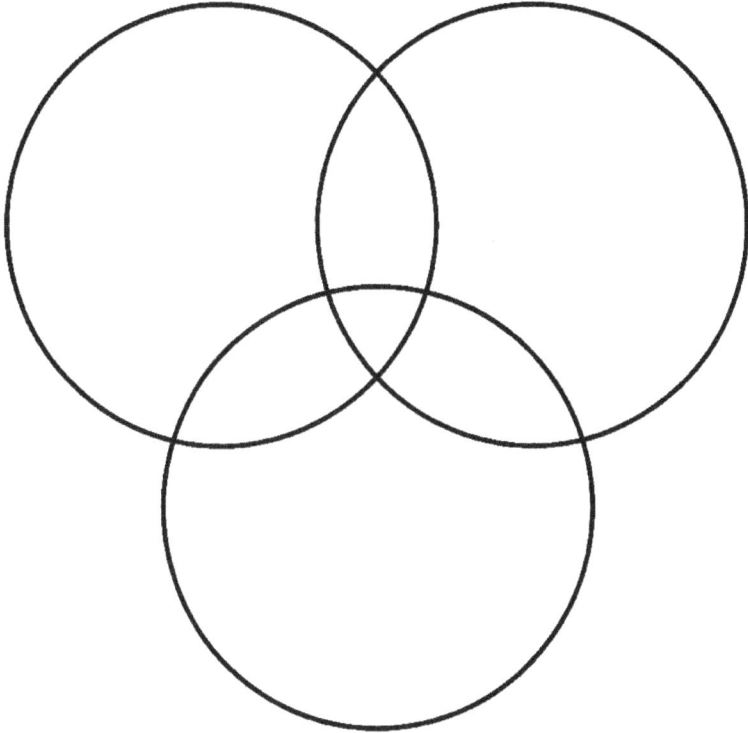

Now, what binds all parts together?

My turn

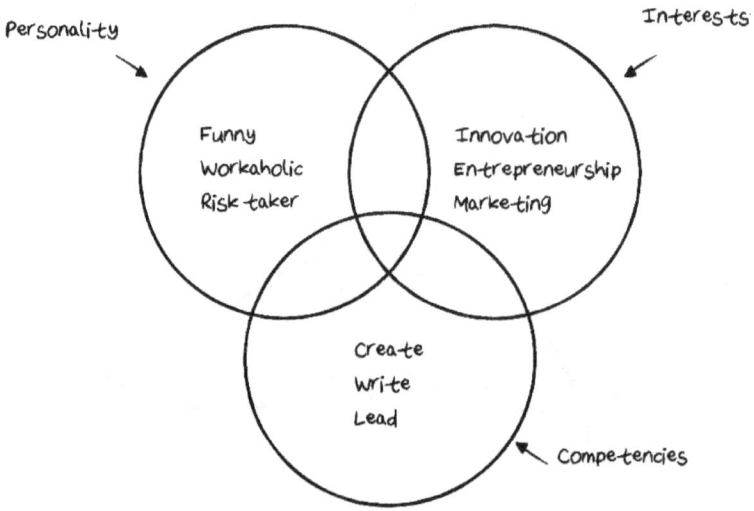

That summarizes who I am. That's my big PIC.

I am:

1. a funny, workaholic risk taker;
2. an innovator, entrepreneur, and marketer; and
3. a creator, writer and leader.

I launched this book on Kickstarter first to:

1. test the idea, test the concept of Shortcuts to Success from A to Z;
2. raise a little bit of money, thanks to 110 backers and around 150 copies sold;

3. get 25 stories of other entrepreneurs to provide some examples to support the theory in every chapter.

Looking at it afterward—I can't say I knew it before or that I did it on purpose, it would be a lie—I realize that this move fits perfectly who I am. Launching my book on Kickstarter was:

1. a funny workaholic risk-taking adventure (nerdy concept, nights & weekends work);
2. an innovative entrepreneur marketing story (at least for a French-Canadian guy);
3. a creative writing and leadership experiment (writing, managing and promoting—those who successfully crowdfund a project can testify).

That leads me to the conclusion that everything you do should fit into your big PIC. As we'll see in the next shortcut, Ctrl-B, your big PIC is made with your life's pillars and contains, at its core, your purpose. So if you ask yourself, "Should I do this?", keep your big PIC in mind before taking any decision. Some people talk about the "flow", while others about the "destiny", the "raison d'etre", "God's will" or "any-other-spiritual-thingy". Call it whatever you want. I don't care. What I care about is your happiness, because unhappy entrepreneurs usually create sad products.

Here are two quotes that I wanted to share with you:

[3]*If we could only take a step back and look, I mean really look, at how we react to situations and interact with other people, we would learn so much about ourselves. It is in this self-awareness that we ultimately find happiness, living life in the "big picture".*

[4]*On a day-to-day basis, your attention is probably on the details: the action steps you need to take to move from A to B and B to C. That's a good thing—this is the level at which work gets done. At times, though, it's vital that you take a step back. It's all too easy to get wrapped up in the little steps of your projects, goals, and even your whole life, without ever thinking much about where you're really heading.*

---

[3] Source: http://www.huffingtonpost.com/donna-labermeier/shift-perspective_b_3202700.html
[4] Source: http://www.pickthebrain.com/blog/why-stepping-back-to-see-the-big-picture-is-so-important/

Your turn

Ctrl-B: **Bold**

Everybody is a genius. But if you judge a fish by its ability to climb a tree, it will live its whole life believing that it is stupid.
- Albert Einstein

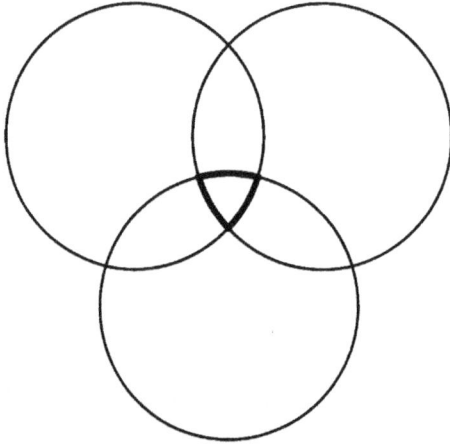

Take a look at your big PIC.

Ask yourself: what constitutes the core at its center?

In other words: what's the glue that holds my circles all together, and, even better, that connects me to the core of people around me?

This is your core. Your bold purpose.

Successful people know that the only way to achieve job satisfaction, which is at the same time the cornerstone of personal satisfaction on a daily basis, is to build around this purpose.

To build the rest of your life around your core means to create something important for you. And for people like you.

That means what you create, a product or a service you care so much about, will meet a need for you and your peers. It will solve a bold problem, not just a fleeting one nobody cares about.

This effort will lead to self-worth, which, once felt, will push you to start over again and again to fight important issues, and to solve bolder problems.

Sooner or later, this feeling of self-worth will become the fuel of your core, every day. And the more you move forward, the bolder your purpose will be.

Finding your core may take time. It may take a lifetime for some people. But let's set a deadline, here. Five minutes. No more.

To get there, see this shortcut as a simple recipe where you have three ingredients that, when combined, produce something greater than the sum of its part— that some call the *dish of a lifetime.*

| Ground Beef | Corn | Potato | Shepherd's pie |

3 ingredients ⟶ 1 core

In Ctrl-A (the previous shortcut), you asked for help from your contacts, family and friends to complete your circles with their feedback. Here, you have to find your own answers. What's your core?

To help you, a good exercise is to take only one word you got per contact earlier to describe your personality, interests and competencies.

Others can obviously help, but it has to come from you—deep within you—because essentially, you face this journey alone.

Without this, you will never have the motivation and the courage to complete the following shortcuts, much less the strength to tackle bold problems only you can solve.

	Contact 1	Contact 2	Contact 3
Personality			
Interests			
Competencies			

What words resonate with you the most?

Once you're done, put only one word in bold in each column of the table above, to mark the importance.

Here are some tips if you struggle with this:

1. Say these words aloud.

2. Draw them.

3. Close your eyes and imagine the picture of what your life would be if you put the emphasis on each word.

4. If you want to go further, write a short story that explains the WHY of each word. 200 words maximum. The shorter the better. Eliminate the words that are not in the story.

So, what is your bold purpose?

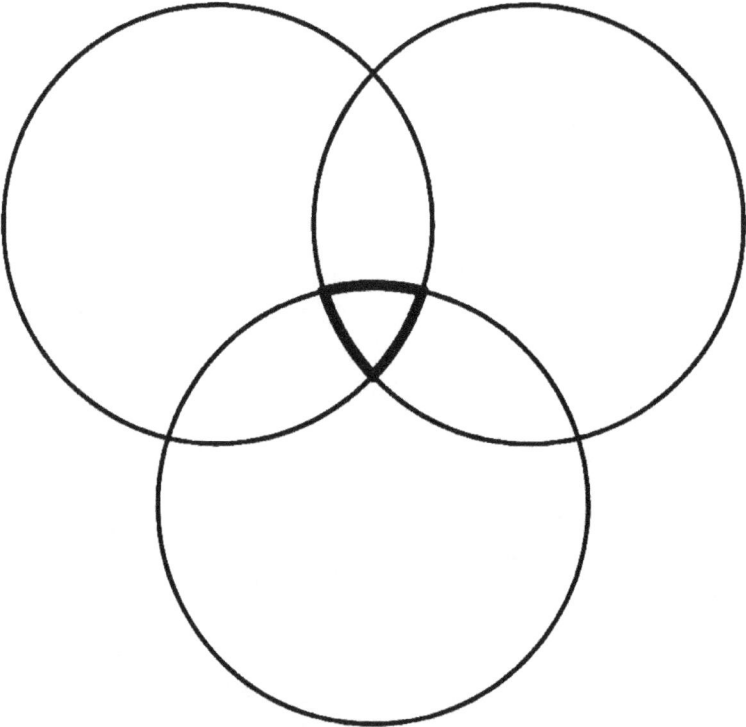

My turn

In the little survey that around 25 people filled out during my Kickstarter campaign, I was asking: "What's your bold purpose? Why do you wake up every morning (or late at night)?"

Honestly, I wake up every morning to feed my cats. What do I do late at night? I plan the next day—except for Tuesday when I watch *The Profit* on CNBC.

The reason I wrote this book was not only to help you reach a "happy success" or "successful happiness", but also to help myself. How selfish can I be?

I wanted to take a pause and make the point with myself.

-   Hold on, little boy! Where the hell are you heading to?

The answer came after some time, but to be honest, it's always evolving, which means the answer today is slightly different from the answer of yesterday. It's not a big variation—I'm not bipolar—but a small variation according to what I'm currently living.

Throughout the funny process of writing this book, I woke up early every morning just to get rid of all the tasks related to my day-to-day job. It's not that I don't like them—far from that—but that the day-to-day routine is usually not what entrepreneurs prefer. You know what I mean?

Once all my tasks were done, I had some free time to work on this book. My purpose was to help other entrepreneurs by creating a light and illustrated business book with simple shortcuts to success and happiness. This book says almost the same things as do other business books, but in a different way. I know there is a need for it. I know it without any market research or big data reports that make me sick. I know it because my friend and like-minded people pre-bought around 150 copies. But beyond all that, I know it because I need it. So I wrote it.

In the same survey, I asked a related question: "What bold problems have you and your business had to solve?"

I think this book aims to solve this problem: being successful and happy at the same time.

To conclude, Socrates once said, "An unexamined life is not worth living". Think about that for a moment...

Then turn the page.

Their turn

Here are some other inspiring answers from my survey to the question: "Why do you wake up every morning?"

I've cut some shorter to really stay focused on the core and make it easier for their purpose to spread. Do the same—it's your turn!

Give real estate a creative thinking approach to marketing.

- Eric Lafontaine, *Founder @ Alliance E.L.*

Push my career a little bit more, every day.

- Jean-Philippe Brousseau, *Web Developer*

To take jobs that have a purpose.

- Raelina Krikston, *Graphic Designer*

Help clients to grow healthy.

- Jennifer Young, *Private Nurse*

Help people recover faster and be healthy and active.

- Annie Kim Lachapelle, *Sport Therapist*

Make a difference in people's lives, one presentation at a time.

- Chantal Bossé, *Presentation Specialist*

Educate people about becoming successful in business thanks to technology.

- Bruce Chamoff, *Blogger @ hotwebideas.net*

Make people's work easier.

- Luce Morin, *Accountant @ activ-ca.ca*

Help people develop new skills that will help them get rid of personal and professional problems.
- Isabelle David, *NLP coach and founder @ IdCom International*

Provide value in the world of entrepreneurship.

- Colin Vincent, *Co-founder @ Equity Directory*

Help people improve their lives so they can change their worlds.

- Alec Tranel, *Founder @ Intern Betas*

Make a difference by thinking out of the box.

- Shahed Kamal, *Founder @ Inovio*

Plug the diversity gap in tech with skill, and the skills gap with diversity.

- Roberta Voulon, *Co-founder @ Hatch Labs*

Digitize cash.

- Moussa Beidas, *Founder @ Bridg*

Make awesome products.

- Heri Rakotomalala, *Product Engineer*

Deliver emotional experiences for a broader range of interests.

- Darryl Wright, *Founder @ Punk Science*

Help small businesses discover how digital marketing can help them.

- Brian Tudor, *Digital Marketer*

Your turn

IDEA

So you want to become an entrepreneur and create a multi-million dollar business?

But what's your idea?

  a) It's the idea of the century! It's going to change the world!
  b) It's a state secret.
  c) I've only talked about this to my spouse, out of fear of being robbed (of the idea, not the spouse).
  d) It's quite complicated to explain.
  e) There is nothing else like it out there.
  f) It solves a new need.
  g) All of the above.
  h) None of the above.

I hope from the bottom of my heart that you have answered H.

Even if you don't have a brilliant idea, it doesn't matter. In fact, there is a good chance that you will never find this brilliant idea. And that's good! Because a genius idea is usually too risky, too ambitious—especially for your first business.

The following shortcuts, Ctrl-C and D, propose you start from what already exists and create an improved copy of it. Quite simple.

Ctrl-C: Copy

To copy is not bad, as taught in school.
This is actually the key to success.

Why, Who and How?

Copy the people you admire

In the previous shortcuts, we saw that, before finding your business idea, you first need to find your core—your bold purpose. If this is not done yet, I would suggest you first copy what the people you admire do:

1. Their lifestyle, cultures and ideals.

2. The way they accomplish great things—their concrete practices. Don't copy the results; they are random and actually a consequence of a mix mainly made of habits, efforts and luck. Copy the process. In neuro-linguistic programming, they talk about the principle of modeling—that is to say, seeing someone's successful behaviours, determining the conditions for success and replicating them.

3. The team that allows them to accomplish great things. Don't make the mistake I would call the *projectors' flaw*, which means to have the projectors focused solely on the person on stage: you. Take a look behind the curtains and discover the hidden forces of the people in the shadow—strengths that complement yours. By surrounding yourself with smart people, you'll

act smartly, no matter what you do. So put the emphasis on the WHO before the WHAT.

4. Their burning desire to be and to do.

5. The way they bounce back, becoming even stronger after failure.

Copy only what fits with your responses to the shortcuts Ctrl-A and B. That means it should stick or be aligned with your big PIC and your bold purpose. Let's exercise together.

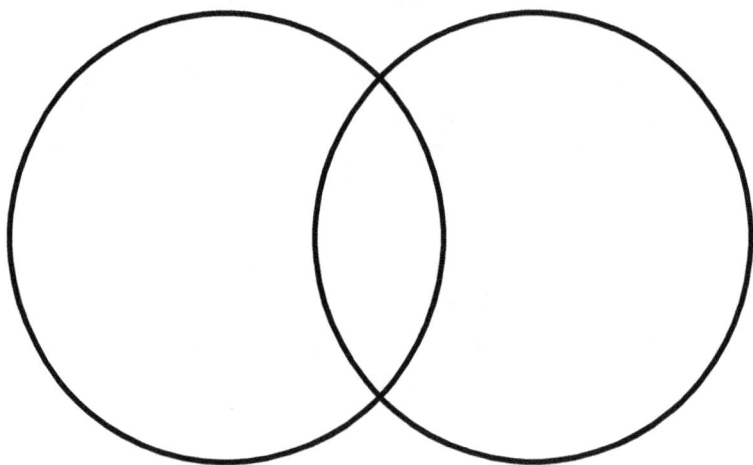

Here are two circles. Simple, right?

In the circle at the left, clip the name of a person you admire or who inspires you.

Very simple.

If you admire this person, this implies that he or she is successful in a particular field—one area that you enjoy and which must necessarily resonate with you. This also implies that this person touches other people like you. This proves the existence of a market for the actions this person takes daily.

Now repeat with another person by inserting his/her name in the circle to the right.

Write the first name that comes to your mind. It does not have to be a known personality. It could be your mentor, your parent, your spouse, your brother or sister, friend, colleague—as long as it is someone who inspires you.

If you lack inspiration, on the next page you will find a list of men and women who inspired (and still inspire) millions of people by the way they concretized their bold purpose and their burning desire to succeed.

100 men and women who inspire millions of people[5]

14th Dalai Lama	Emperor Constantine	Lech Walesa	Pope John Paul II
Abraham Lincoln Lincoln	Ernest Hemingway	Leo Tolstoy	Princess Diana
Adolf Hitler	Eva Peron	Leonardo da Vinci	Queen Victoria
Akbar	Franklin D. Roosevelt	Lord Buddha	Ramses II
Albert Einstein	Galileo Galilei	Louis Pasteur	Rosa Parks
Alexander Fleming	Genghis Kahn	Lyndon Johnson	Saladin
Alexander the Great	George Orwell	Mahatma Gandhi	Samuel Johnson
Aristotle	George Washington	Malcolm X	Sigmund Freud
Ataturk	Giuseppe Garibaldi	Marcus Aurelius	Simon Bolivar
Aung San Suu Kyi	Guru Nanak	Margaret Thatcher	Sir Isaac Newton
Babur	Haile Selassie	Marie Curie	Sir Walter Raleigh
Beethoven	Henry Ford	Martin Luther	Socrates
Benazir Bhutto	Indira Gandhi	Martin Luther King, Jr.	Sri Krishna
Benjamin Franklin	Johann Sebastian Bach	Mikhail Gorbachev	St Paul
Bill Gates	Jawaharlal Nehru	Mohammed Ali	Susan B. Anthony
Boris Yeltsin	Jesus Christ	Mother Teresa	Thomas Edison
Catherine the Great	Joan of Arc	Mozart	Thomas Jefferson
Charlemagne	Johann Gutenberg	Muhammad	Tim Berners Lee
Charles Darwin	John F. Kennedy	Napoleon Bonaparte	Vladimir Lenin
Charles de Gaulle	John Lennon	Nelson Mandela	Voltaire
Christopher Columbus	John M Keynes	Nikola Tesla	William Shakespeare
Confucius	Joseph Stalin	Oliver Cromwell	William Tyndale
Dr. BR Ambedkar	Karl Marx	Oscar Wilde	William Wilberforce
Dwight Eisenhower	Kofi Annan	Pablo Picasso	Winston Churchill
Eleanor Roosevelt	Konrad Adenauer	Plato	Woodrow Wilson

If you want a more business-focused list, turn the page.

---

[5] Source: http://www.biographyonline.net/people/people-who-changed-world.html

50 of the greatest business leaders of the 20th century[6]

Alfred P. Sloan, Jr. - General Motors	John F. Welch, Jr. - General Electric
Andrew S. Grove - Intel	John P. Morgan - J.P. Morgan Chase
Asa G. Candler - Coca-Cola	John T. Dorrance - Campbell Soup
Charles R. Schwab - Charles Schwab	Leon L. Bean - LL Bean
Clarence Birdseye - Bird's Eye Foods	Michael Dell - Dell
Daniel F. Gerber, Jr. - Gerber Products	Milton S. Hershey - The Hershey Co.
David Packard - Hewlett-Packard	Philip H. Knight - Nike
David Sarnoff - RCA	Raymond A. Kroc - McDonald's
Estee Lauder - Estee Lauder	Robert (Ted) E. Turner - Turner Broadcasting
Frederick W. Smith - Federal Express	Robert W. Johnson, Jr. - Johnson & Johnson
George Eastman - Eastman Kodak	Samuel M. Walton - Walmart
Gordon E. Moore - Intel	Steven P. Jobs - Apple
Harland Sanders - Kentucky Fried Chicken	Thomas J. Watson, Jr - IBM
Henry Ford - Ford Motor	Thomas J. Watson, Sr - IBM
Henry J. Heinz - Heinz	Walter A. Haas, Jr. - Levi Strauss
Henry J. Kaiser - Kaiser Industries	Walter A. Haas, Sr. - Levi Strauss
Henry R. Luce - Time-Life Publications	Walter E. Disney - Walt Disney
Herbert D. Kelleher - Southwest Airlines	Warren E. Buffett - Berkshire Hathaway
Howard Schultz - Starbucks	Will K. Kellogg - Kellogg
J. Willard Marriott, Jr. - Marriott Int'l	William C. Procter - Procter & Gamble
James E. Burke - Johnson & Johnson	William E. Boeing - Boeing
James E. Casey - United Parcel Service	William H. Gates III - Microsoft
James L. Kraft - Kraft Foods	William Levitt - Levitt & Sons
James O. McKinsey - McKinsey & Co	William R. Hewlett - Hewlett-Packard
John D. Rockefeller, Sr. - Standard Oil	William Wrigley, Jr. - Wm. Wrigley Jr. Co.

How are these two people similar? Why do they inspire you? Is their core like yours?

If you have several people who inspire you, you can create other circles and do the same exercise. Being limited to two people helps you see more clearly and not be scattered.

Comparing yourself to people you admire, people who are successful in a given market, will help you discover what you want to do, find the actions that will lead you to the best of yourself and, above all, will position yourself on your WHY.

---

[6] Source: http://www.fastcompany.com/53477/greatest-business-leaders-20th-century

Why do you want to do this, or accomplish that? Why do you want to devote your life to it, at least for the next three years?

The answer to the WHY is the source of motivation you need to lead your project to completion, regardless of the nature and scale of this project.

Remember how they taught you to build a sentence in grade school?

WHO + WHAT + WHY/TO WHOM/HOW

In the school model, the WHY exists as part of the group of modifiers to make nicer sentences, but it is still just a modifier, and teachers will tell you it is optional, by definition.

What schools miss is one of the main reasons why sentences and words exist: to inspire actions.

That's especially true in business. And that's exactly what inspires the people you admire.

By looking carefully at the five things to copy from those mentioned earlier, you will notice the syntax to create a business is a little bit different. Here it is:

WHY + WHO + HOW

For example:

To help entrepreneurs	Steve Blank	creates useful content
WHY	WHO	HOW

The WHY sparks the action. It's the reason you wake up every morning. It's the glue that makes the WHO and the HOW stick together. By the way: if your WHY is to make money, you probably overlooked shortcuts Ctrl-A and B. And you probably won't make a lot of money.

The WHO is you and your team. WHO do you need to accomplish your WHY? What key strengths do you have? Which key players do you have? You can start the ride alone, for sure—but as you grow, you will have to surround yourself with people smarter than you.

The HOW is the way you deliver your business promise. How do you serve your why? What's your value proposition? Maybe you already have a clear idea of the business and product you want to build, so your HOW will be precise and concrete. Maybe you don't. And that's just fine!

Wonder why there's no WHAT? It's because the WHAT can wait. While many people may be confused by the difference between the HOW and the WHAT, the WHAT is a consequence of the WHY + WHO + HOW. It's the outcome of the process, the meal created by the recipe. The WHAT is constantly changing, because things evolve fast, as are markets and people's needs. We all are greedy; we continuously want new, fresh, cool things. What's in today is out tomorrow.

So is your WHAT.

Too many young entrepreneurs find the WHAT at first, make the mistake of falling in love with it, go bankrupt with it... and go back to their corporate jobs. Fall in love with your WHY, not with your WHAT. If I have one piece of advice to give, that would be it.

- I want to create the next greatest mobile app.
- Why? How? And who? You don't care about technology, you don't have a clue about programming, and you don't know anyone who does.

First things first: know your WHY. Then your WHO. Finally, find your HOW.

We usually talk about the three P's of business at its core: People, Process, Product.

I think this is exactly the right order of importance. The People incorporate the WHY and the WHO; the Process is the HOW and the Product is the WHAT.

From the moment you fix that, you'll discover tons of possibilities for your WHAT. For example, Steve Blank's WHATs are, to name a few: books, blog posts, interviews, conferences, seminars, webinars, software, receptions.

I know it may be hard to re-learn how to build a sentence. That's why you should practice a bit. Building a business should be as *hard* as building straight-to-the-point sentences.

First, write down what the people you admire do.

	Why	Who	How
Idol 1			
Idol 2			

Then it's your turn. What's the sentence that will lead your success story? What's the sentence that will inspire you to move forward, no matter how hard it is?

	Why	Who	How
You			

There you go! You now have the path to follow to launch your first business, summed up in one simple statement. At the same time, it is your sales pitch to potential customers, employees and investors! It's short and sweet, easy to remember and easy for word of mouth to spread.

What?

Copy what people want

Now that you have found your key WHY + WHO + HOW sentence, you need to find the WHAT—something concrete. Let's call it a product. Here's a simple step by step process to create a product that I call the *ice cream way of building a delicious product.*

Copy an existing product

A successful product proves there is a market for it. By copying the product idea (the idea only, not the product itself), you are on the right path to creating a product that people will buy. Actually, you could take this simple strategy: travel (or simply Google it) and discover products that work in other countries and adapt them to your local market, or copy a product that exists in an industry and adapt it to another use and/or to another industry.

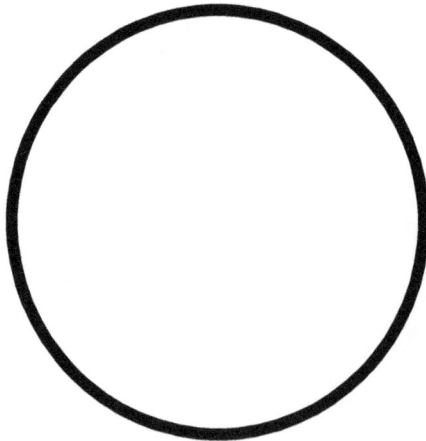

In a growing market

Your product idea could be great, but if your market is dying (or worse, if it doesn't exist), no matter how many features and how much bling-bling your product has, nobody will care!

Most entrepreneurs stop here. They find product to copy and a growing market, and are satisfied because they have a business that generates profits.

Unfortunately, few people care about these businesses, just as few people get excited about a single-scoop ice cream cone. They look the same as their competitors and people never talk about them during dinner. They are boring, so to speak. Thank God there are two other simple things you can do to go from boring to great.

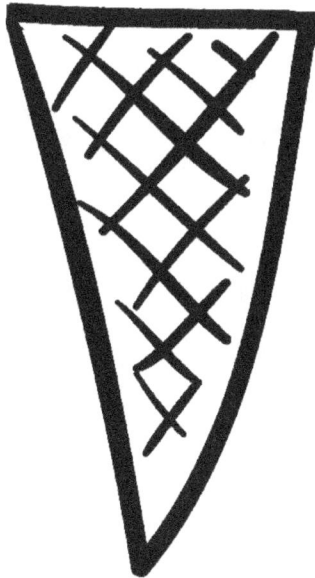

Combine your product idea with your core

You think you have a product that will sell. But how much will you care about this product? How much effort will you put into selling it? Would you sell one to yourself? Hence the relevance of combining the product idea with your core, so it meets your bold purpose. That is what will motivate you to get up in the morning, to put all your sweat into it and to create the most amazing product on earth.

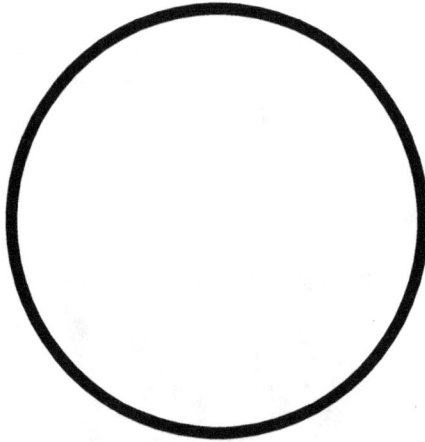

Improve the product with a little twist

Your product will matter for you, and that's great! But will it be a hit or a flop? Will it sell a lot?

To sell more, your product idea needs to be remarkable. It needs a little twist. Be careful, though: to improve the product with a little twist doesn't necessarily mean adding something to the product. It could be related to the product, of course, but it could be to simplify it, to better define its use or to remove a feature. Or it could be related to something around the product, like the business model, the way to sell it, the marketing or the use of the product in a new market for a new function... Whatever, as long as the product better serves target customers.

The ice cream way of building a delicious product

The theory above looks great, doesn't it?

But in practice, to find a great product idea is not that simple. That's why, like everything else, the key is to practice.

Here are the circles of WHAT. I know, that's a lot of circles, but it's worth it. Try it.

What's your product?

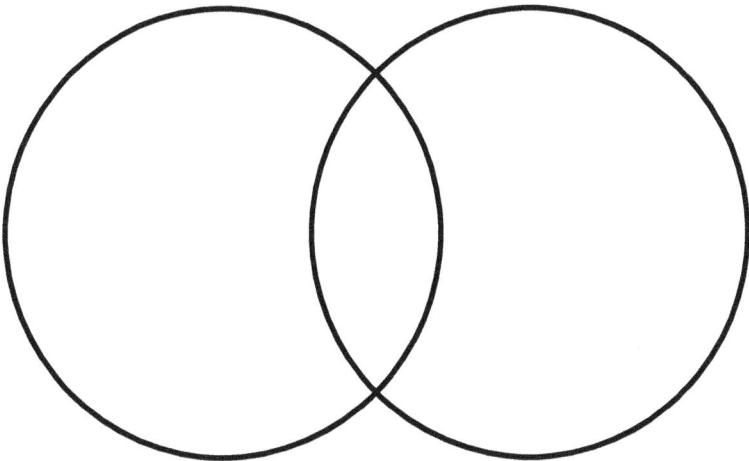

In the circle on the left, insert the name of something you love, like a product, a service or a passion that excites you and that you would be willing to pay for.

Anything.

Again, if you love this thing—I mean truly love it— there are other people similar to you who love it, too.

Thus, we validate the existence of a need—an essential exercise before getting into any project, yet so often overlooked by young entrepreneurs, and even by the most experienced ones. Besides, do you know the most dangerous word for an entrepreneur?

To guess.

It is neither fear nor risk, which are only the consequences of the assumptions you've made when you guessed.

In the circle on the right, insert another thing you love. It doesn't have to be related to the first thing. Actually, it's best when it's completely different, to combine unexpected things. It could be anything: a product, a hobby, a business model, a service, a cool design, a weird object, a grandmother's recipe—anything.

The only requirement is that it is a passion for you and resonates with you.

Of course, you may not find all the responses overnight. I'm aware of that. But give it a shot. Go with your gut feeling. If you struggle, do this exercise: combine two random things to create a new, third one.

This third thing is usually a nice surprise. Actually, the more random and different the two initial things are, the bigger the surprise is. And that *surprise effect* is exactly what attracts the market's attention because it is new, remarkable and unexpected.

That being said, when I'm referring to a *surprise effect*, I don't mean creating a show with fireworks and rainbows. I want you to keep it as simple as possible—always.

Note how the best ideas are the simplest. Your idea should be simple, too. Barely stupid would be awesome.

Man + Woman = Baby   ——————▶   Surprise!

Is there anything that attracts more people's attention than a cute little baby?

"That's stupid!" some serious business people will say—ones too serious to actually innovate.

Well, that's not stupid at all.

You might be surprised to learn that most of the innovations that have had huge success have been discovered thanks to this stupid little exercise of combining two random things to create a third, new thing.

This is what I call *stuplicity*: the mix of stupidity and simplicity.

Stuplicity is what allows, generates and feeds word of mouth because something simple and stupid is easy to remember. It's actually the thing you remember the most, most of the time. It's so easy to talk about with the office colleagues or at dinner with family or through social media. And that's really entertaining!

If you add *stuplicity* to copying two existing things that work to create a new one, you end up with a killer formula.

The outcome is as simple as it is stupid: easy to remember and easy to spread. And because you copy two existing things, customers are not scared by it. Even if it's new, the product reminds people of two existing ones they know. So it's an innovation that's easy to swallow, with a familiar face, which makes customers feel safe and makes the sale *easy* to close.

Here are some examples of things that were combined to create a third, new one. I'll just throw a few of them out, sorted by category.

2 sports: Wakeboard + Parachute = Kitesurfing

2 products: Television + Computer = Apple TV

2 services: Video club + Internet = Netflix

2 jobs: Programmer + Designer = Web designer

2 foods: Peanut butter + Chocolate = Reese's

2 activities: Taking pictures + Socializing = Instagram

2 websites: Flickr + Facebook = Instagram

2 ideologies: Communism + Capitalism = China

2 different categories (a service and a process): Restaurant + Assembly line = McDonald's

The list could go into considerably more depth... as far as copying an existing, proven and successful idea and applying it to another market.

For example: let's take Tinder, the popular dating app:

Tinder for Product Hunt = ProducTind

Tinder for content = Daily, by Buffer

Tinder for news = iQ news

Tinder for Reddit = Karma Swipe

Tinder for dogs = BarkBuddy

Tinder for threesomes = 3nder

Tinder for business networking = Grip, Weave, CoffeeMe, Caliber

Tinder for jobs = Blonk, Emjoyment, Jobr

Tinder for finding new music = SongHop

Tinder for shopping shoes online = Shoe Swipe

Tinder for discovering new products = Mallzee

Tinder for dresses = Namechange

Tinder for Jewish people = JSwipe

Tinder for older adults = Stitch

Tinder for deals = Kwoller

Tinder for programmers = Girt

Tinder for unfollowing Twitter users = Twindr

Tinder for *[fill in the blank]* = *[find a cool name]*

There is even a site to mashup two well-known startups together randomly to create a new one. It's here: www.startupbreeding.com

The list could go even further to combine a thing and its opposite:

Fast Food + the opposite = Slow Food

Redbull + the opposite = Slow Cow

Winter jacket + the opposite = Swimming suit

Buying a car + the opposite = Uber

Anyway... you got it, right?

You can draw as many circles as you'd like, pell-mell, and then assemble them two-by-two, trying the different possible combinations to create a third, unexpected thing.

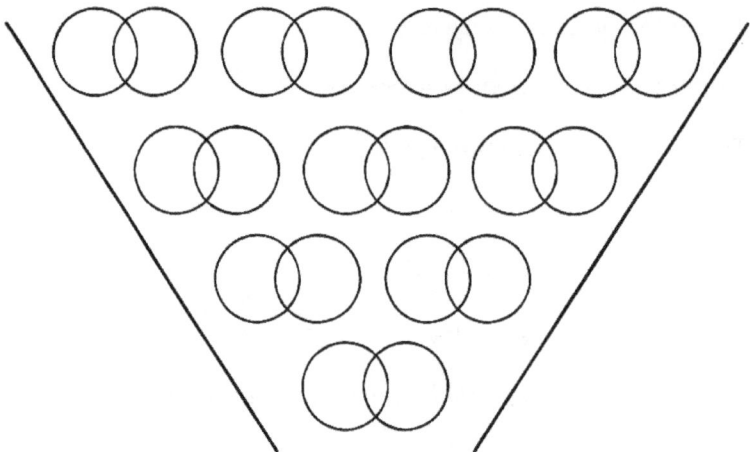

However, you ideally want to keep this as simple as possible: at the moment, what resonates with you, coincides with your bold purpose and meets the needs of an existing market?

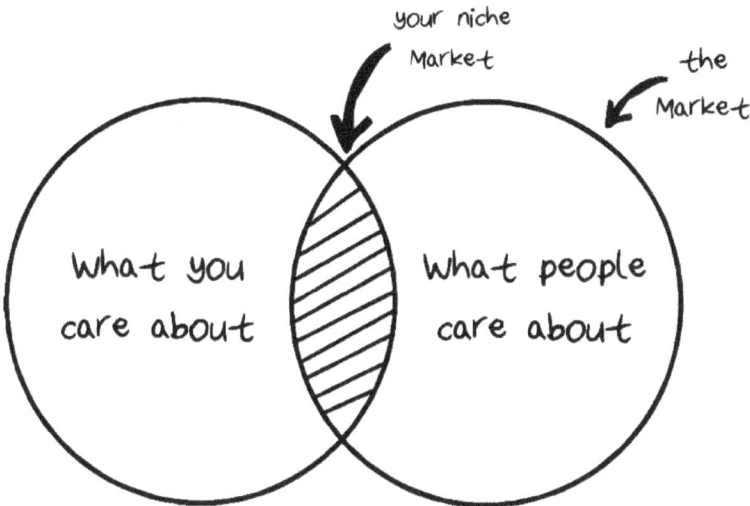

A lot of water can flow under the bridge before it comes to you... but don't think you can sit and wait for the idea of the century to come. It will not come!

In fact, the coward rarely screams, "Eureka!"

In the absence of the genius idea you're expecting, what do you have? What did you do until now?

You have identified your core, to which you must rally the future brilliant idea to motivate you in the long term. That is the key to professional success that will allow you to see and seize opportunities as they arise. This actually illustrates the process of how you can find your genius idea—not the other way around.

In school, you are taught that copying is wrong and that plagiarism is a serious offense, punishable by expulsion. But in reality, everything is just a copy of something else: bad copies die, while improved copies survive.

My turn

- Hey Derek, let's copy some best-selling books to create a best-selling book!

That's what I told myself when I started this. What an astounding idea! No, seriously, it was. I mean, if you have the choice to copy a great product or a bad product, what do you choose?

So, I've looked at the really successful books I've read and at the reviews on Amazon to know what people liked and disliked about them. I had a few inspirations that shaped my life until today, like:

- *The 4-hour workweek*, especially the simple D-E-A-L concept through which Tim Ferriss explain an *easy* path to make good money and live a free and joyful life.
- *The Art of Start* by Guy Kawasaki, especially because it's a simple step-by-step approach to launching a business, and it answers every question you might have.
- *The $100 Startup*, because it breaks the myth that you need money to start a business. In his book, the author Chris Guillebeau shows with tons of stories what you really need to start a business and to live from it, that I'd call the 3 P's: purpose, passion, profit.

But the books I copied the most are:

- *Business Model Generation*, from Alex Osterwalder and Yves Pigneur
    - By extension *Business Model You,* co-written by the two authors above along with Tim Clark.
- *The Lean Startup,* from Eric Ries

I took from the first one the focus on the visual aspect, the simple doodle-like illustrations and the simple business model canvas. In short, the fun and refreshing perspective on business.

I took from the second one the "Lean" aspect, the approach to quickly build a product, test and iterate fast, learn from all the process and pivot when necessary. Actually, the process that the world of startups uses—often seen as too techy or innovative for *normal* people and *normal* businesses—should be taught to every business owner. In short, I took from *The Lean Startup* the concept that encapsulates the way running a business should be.

Their turn

From all the answers I got to my survey question "Who inspires you? What actions, ideas or business did you (partially) copy?", I was amazed by the variety of sources of inspiration. I was expecting a lot of Steve Jobs, Elon Musk or Richard Branson. I had some, of course! But overall, I found out that people are inspired by other people I don't know! And that's cool because it brings diversity to another level, from which emerges more surprising startups. Love it!

To inspire you, here's the TOP 10 I curated from my homemade survey, in a random order:

1. Vince Mcmahon and Donald Trump. Both marketing geniuses, they are focusing their energy on building their brand and sticking to it. I learned from them that you need to inspire people with stories.

2. My father always inspired me to be self-employed and to be an entrepreneur. I always wanted to follow in his footsteps for results but do it my way to be original.

3. My partners and my enemies inspire me. I learn with each of their moves, good or bad.

4. People who think outside the box and have the vision to build a better world. The Walt Disney philosophy about "guest experience" has inspired us for a long time.

5. Great people from the NLP and hypnotherapy field, like John Grinder, Richard Bandler, Robert Dilts,

Judith DeLozier, Milton Erickson, Ernest Rossi, Alfred Korzybski, Abraham Maslow, etc. But also people from other personal growth fields like Deepak Chopra, Eckhart Tolle, Arnaud Desjardins and many more!

6. IDEO. They have been one of the oldest and brightest beacons for "good design" since their inception, and I commend them for it.

7. I am beyond inspired by Elon Musk. He is an alien, and I love him for that. I love James Dean because he's a badass. And Gandhi.

8. Lots of role models (Dr. Bill Miller of SRI/Stanford, Bob Bishop of SGI, Ed Blechschmidt of Unisys, Laura Kilcrease of Austin, Reto Braun of Unisys, my wife).

9. I am inspired by studios like Square Enix, Valve, Naughty Dog, Pixelnauts, Supercell and even Netflix for their approach to human values.

10. Kevin Rose was an early "hero". I have followed his growth.

Now it's your turn! Whom and what should you copy? Come on, do it!

Your turn

Ctrl-D: Style

You may not have a clue about your improved copy idea.

This is normal. Have no fear.

Start from there.

The key is to:

1. Keep the idea simple.

2. Create a copy of something that already works.

3. Combine it with your core.

4. Make it meet your bold purpose.

5. Enhance it to create an improved copy.

You should aim to create a copy that will work even better than the original one, and which, thanks to the snowball effect, will generate the best of yourself—focusing on and aligning with your bold purpose—and will maximize the added value you create for customers.

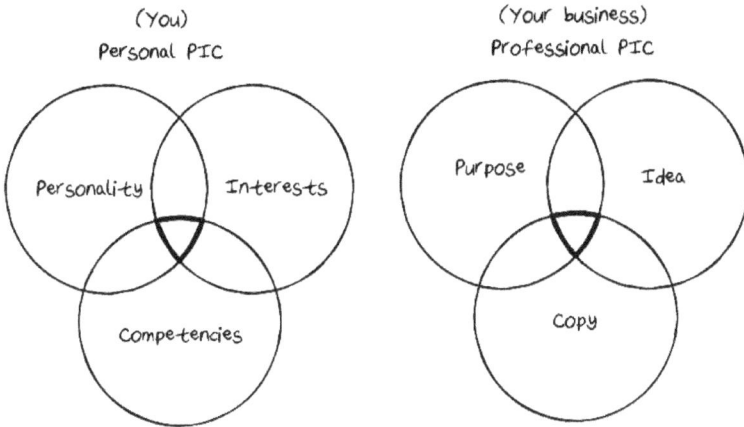

(You)
Personal PIC

Personality   Interests

Competencies

(Your business)
Professional PIC

Purpose   Idea

Copy

Now how can you determine the value you and your business create?

There are three factors:

1. The Price
2. The Service
3. The Style

The vast majority of companies focus on the first two: the price and the service. And they pretend to stand out from competitors as well.

Some entrepreneurs will copy an existing business that works and lower the price or improve the service, or both. And they believe they've created an improved copy. However, the actual improved copy does not improve only the price and the service. It also improves the copy to the root by improving the idea, the concept, the business model and all other organs connected directly or indirectly to the product itself. In short, it improves the Style.

To explain what I mean by Style, with a capital S, let's take the example of a new catering company that attempts to differentiate itself on the basis of its industry-leading prices and better customer service.

How does the catering company really differentiate itself from its competitors? Classy people prefer to pay more for a caterer with a certain reputation and will expect top-quality service. People who want to pay less either not afford a caterer, either pay what they can, and still, they expect top-quality service. They pay for a caterer; after all, it's normal to expect the best service!

The moral of this story? The new caterer is doomed never to become #1 on the market if he does not appeal to the Style.

Style is not about aesthetics—don't be confused. Style is about the business design—its purpose, idea, concept, business model, revenue streams, cost structure, partners, customer segments, channels, logistics, marketing, any of its internal and external communications and all interactions of the company's members with customers.

The Style is the identity of your improved copy to which customers will adhere. Some call it the brand, but it's not that. The Style goes beyond the brand.

The Style is the key ingredient that will allow you to create an improved copy of a successful product, impregnated by your core and led by your bold purpose, which will stick to the daily habits of target customers.

Let's take a simple example.

Suppose you have a knee problem. Will you see a doctor or a knee doctor?

Both are doctors, but one targets a different customer segment. And guess what? You're right in this segment!

Let me ask a question now: who has more clients? The doctor or the knee doctor?

- The doctor's targets are broader, one might reason, so the doctor would have more potential clients!
- Are you sure about that?

You better have the right target, a narrower one, easy to identify, and the right weapon—like a sneaky, cost-effective sniper who shoots one perfectly precise bullet at a time, instead of a shotgun that shoots everyone and scares the hell out of every potential customer.

Let's dig into a less scary and more detailed example.

Suppose the company you want to create is selling shoes. The market for shoes is illustrated by the circle below:

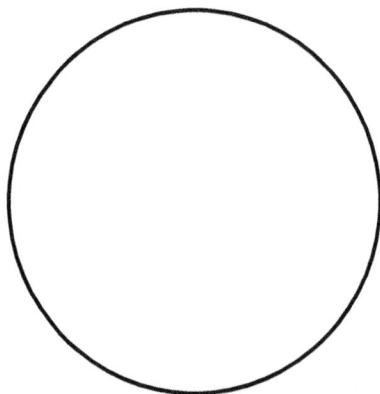

To compete with the big players out there, you should target a tight niche market that is currently badly served and/or that you will serve in a new and better manner, with an improved copy that will help you gain market shares quickly.

So, target a small market where you could be the best, or at least be better positioned with a clear message that speaks directly to the people similar to you. A small market in which you will have a competitive advantage: to swim in it daily and to know it better than anyone else.

One of the most hurtful, mistaken beliefs that kills a business even before it starts is this one: if you serve a big market with a lot of people, you will have more chances to find customers.

That's wrong.

The more narrow your market, the more you target a niche; the less you have potential customers in numbers, the more you know WHO your targets are, their gender, age, mindset, interests, where they hang out, their hobbies, where they work, where they live, what they eat...ok, I think you got it. You're not the CIA, and you won't spy on them. But you know what? You should.

This brings us back to the doctor and the knee doctor. Or the guy that hunts the moon with a shotgun.

The more you are focused on pleasing a tight niche market in a new and better way, the better your chances are at attracting a lot of customers quickly. By the way, the word *quickly* is really important here because time and timing are the most important factors of success when you launch a business, more than the execution, the idea or the funding.

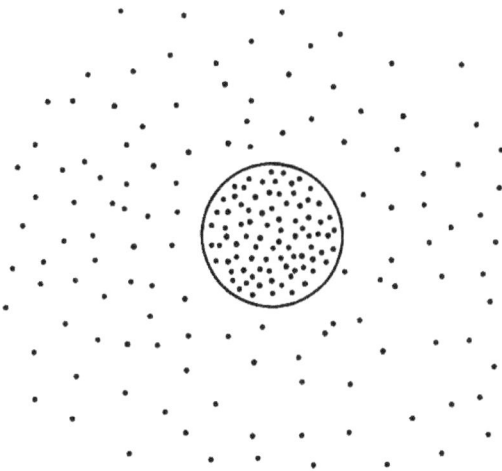

Overall, there are two ways to target:

1. Location (for example, the hair salon in your neighborhood)
2. Value proposition (what you offer to customers)

In an ideal world, a smart business strategy would be to combine both a great location (geographic advantage) and a unique value proposition (product advantage). But this is not always possible or necessary.

Let's go back to our shoes market example and target a bit more. Let's take the golf shoes market (the value proposition) in Montreal (the location).

However, let's specify that the more you target for the value proposition, the more you can aspire to an international market, and then the less you have to care about the location. Actually, the value proposition and the location are the poles of the same axis.

Value proposition ———————————————————— Location

The more you tend to go toward one side, the more you can *neglect* the other side*.

That being said, testing a "high value proposition" product locally first is usually a smart strategy to avoid drowning in a global market in which you have never swum.

For example, whether you launch a hair salon, a drug store or a mini-market similar to the one next door, it's all about three things: location, location and location.

Value
proposition ————————————————————————(here)—— Location

On the other side, if you launch a tech product, a mobile app or a new fashion trend not similar to anything else that exists on earth, it's all about the value proposition and going worldwide.

Value
proposition ——(here)———————————————————————— Location

What if you launch a hair salon, a drug store or a mini-market with a twist in its Style: a different business model, a new revenue stream, a new cost-effective way to run the store, a new way to display products, a new interior design and layout, a new technology, a new process—actually anything you can imagine to make it a greater business that attracts more customers and makes more money. A business that sits right in the middle of the Value proposition/Location axis.

Value
proposition ————————————————(here)———————————— Location

Guess what, maybe you could create franchises after you've proven the first location thrives?

Let's go ahead with the golf shoes market and get rid of location for this example because it's irrelevant and a suicidal strategy here.

Even though the golf shoes market is a lot smaller than the shoes market, it still is a large market with plenty of big sharks that are well established. The ideal situation would be to target even more—let's say the orthopedic golf shoes market, for example.

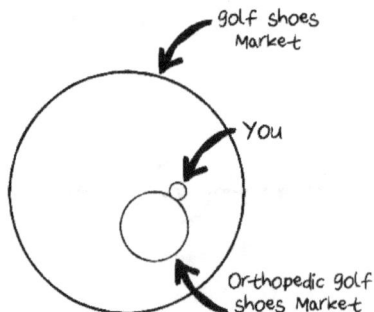

Quick note here. If you target the keyword "orthopedic golf shoes" versus the keyword "shoes", what are your chances to rank on Google's first page?

If you choose "shoes", I hope you have deep pockets with unlimited funds to beat Nike, Adidas and the other big guns spending billions in search engine optimization, marketing and advertising.

Logically, if you want to get inside this tight niche market, you have to penetrate to the extremity of the perimeter. Imagine the perimeter of the market as a circle with a rigid circumference. In fact, the circumference is really solid; that's what we call the entry barriers, that protect (to a certain point) the companies already inside the circle to keep the market shares away from a newcomer.

So, you must break through the barrier of the circle to get inside. But how?

The best way—and actually the only way Adam Smith, the capitalist father of the pure and perfect concurrence, would approve—is to create an improved copy that will satisfy more of the needs of the customers that already buy orthopedic golf shoes.

In brief, to innovate.

However, to innovate and have success are two completely different things. That's why your innovation, to both innovate and succeed, must be born at the margin of the market it conquers (illustration #3 below).

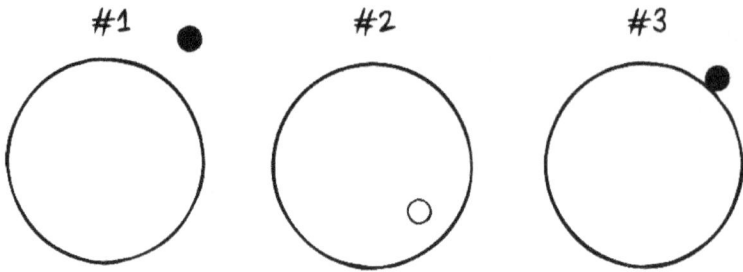

#1   **#2**   **#3**

Illustration #1: Too much innovation
As the lives of Tesla or Leonardo da Vinci demonstrate, an innovation too big for its time or too far from the market can't be understood or adopted by a market of customers reluctant to change and slow to change their habits. How many great ideas have known success only decades after their creators died?

Illustration #2: Too little innovation
An innovation that is too small doesn't have enough time to grow; it gets killed in the egg, gets eaten in one bite by a competitor or gets ignored by the market. Too little innovation ends up short-lived, or an already expired, copy-pasted product that loses itself in the mass of similar products and is swallowed up by big sharks. Or it simply keeps people indifferent, which is the worst possible scenario.

Illustration #3: Innovation at the margin
An innovation at the margin of the market is the perfect type. Not too little nor too much, the innovation expands little by little, like the embryo, thanks to the push toward the center of the circle by the customers who want more and more of this. The embryo feeds itself with the competitors' shares of the pie.

Here is an illustrated summary of the process for getting into a market.

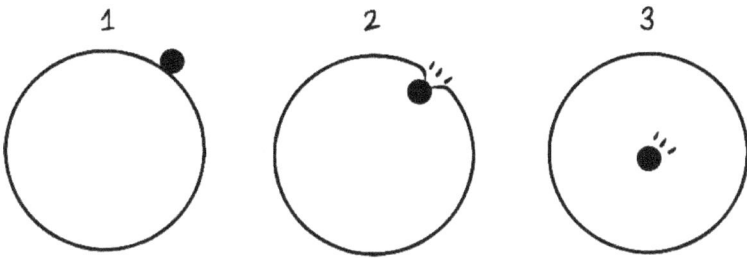

1. Choose a niche market. Offer an improved copy to customers of something that exists and is also easily recognizable to them. Position yourself at the margin of this market. Take advantage of the negligence of your competitors who won't care about you or won't see you on their radar; improve on things they are too busy to acknowledge, or things overlooked because of a lack of vision by their leaders.

2. Let yourself be absorbed by the people who will marry your Style little by little. Improve your copy by listening to their needs and feedback. Your Style must adapt itself and be more refined when in touch with the target customers. Be customer-driven.

3. Sprint. Attack the heart of this niche market and redefine the rules of the game with your Style.

"What a nice theory!" This is what you're probably thinking.

But I guess that you still don't know how to create your improved copy, do you?

Zoom inside the circle of your copy to define its Style—a Style that will stick to customers' needs and will create an improved copy.

To make it so, you need to be this customer, somehow—to be in his or her skin and live like him or her.

The exercise of the empathy wheel, more known as the empathy map, will help you become that customer you target. It consists of observing the heart of your niche market and identifying the customer—you need to find a name, a job, and all the other characteristics that specify who he or she is, talks to, thinks, feels, says, does, sees, hears, his/her top three pains, and his/her top three gains.

Get out, in the street; go meet potential customers face to face, and observe them.

To have a unique Style, use all of your senses and all of the senses of the copy you're improving. Without that, its identity won't be complete, and people won't adhere to it. The attraction force toward the heart of the niche market won't exist. And the project will die inside the egg.

The Empathy Wheel

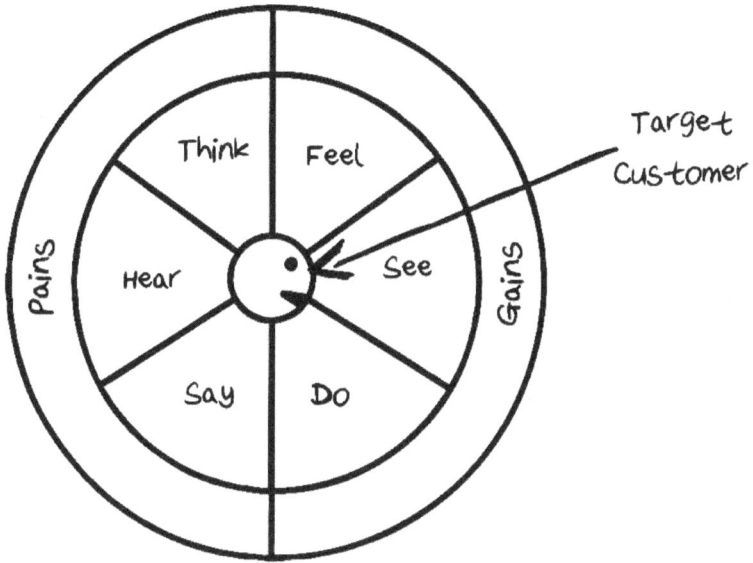

My turn

Now that you know that I copied some books, do you want to throw some tomatoes or some flowers at me? I love both, anyway.

You know, I did exactly what they told us not to do at school. And guess what? It worked! The proof is that you made it until now (reading these lines).

Now that I had a good copy, I needed something better—an improved copy.

Beyond the copy, what makes this book great—or good or at least different—is the new ingredients added to the recipes of success tested and proved by the authors and books that I copied. In short, its Style. Here's the basics of it, the four main ingredients:

1. The first ingredient of its Style is born of a constraint, which is one of the most powerful factors of innovation. The constraint is to use the keyboard shortcuts from Ctrl A to Z as an analogy of a step-by-step path to success and happiness.

This constraint enticed me like I had never been enticed before. You see, I spend most of my days on my computer working or lurking for news about startups and cool stuff. I knew very few keyboard shortcuts and even fewer shortcuts to success, since I still wasn't very successful—at least in the way the "Go Big or Fail Big" American Dream fans from Texas would define success.

So instead of watching TV, playing games or counting the hours while my girlfriend is working, I decided to jump into it and dig deeper.

2. The second ingredient is the *stuplicity*, which is creating something as simple as stupid. That's why I created simple illustrations, short chapters, sleek design and wrote in plain English. OK, that, I have to admit, is due to the fact I'm French-speaking and far from being bilingual.

I wanted to write a book my children would understand, I mean before it's too late, before schools burn their minds and rob their souls.

People these days don't have time to read books—half pretend to be too busy, half too lazy. I fall into both categories. You?

3. The third ingredient is the Kickstarter campaign. As mentioned in this Ctrl-D shortcut, the Style is not limited to the product you sell, but to everything that surrounds it. The example of the Octopus illustrates what I mean about the Style.

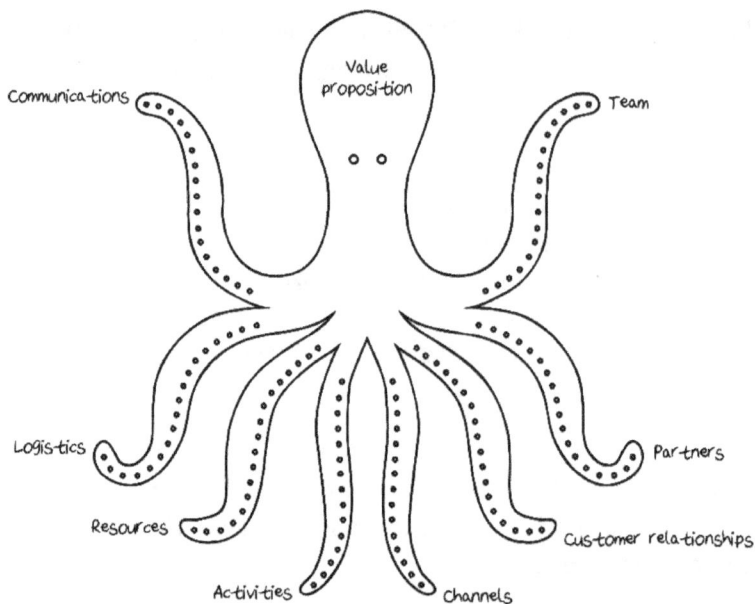

What was so great about the crowdfunding campaign was that it made my Octopus stronger on every leg, and then made my Style stronger (more unique, stylish and refined).

4. The fourth ingredient, intimately tied to the Style, is the business model. We will discuss that later.

I've talked enough; now it's your turn! What is your Style?

Their turn

Here are the top 12 answers from my survey to the question: "How did you create an improved copy of something that already existed? What is the Style of your business?"

1. My company's main focus is on realtors that are not experiencing great sales growth in the luxury real estate segment in Montreal. We create memorable experiences for their customers and make sure storytelling is at the heart of their marketing.

2. By listening to my client and giving them what they really want. It's not about saying yes to everything that they want. It's about helping them achieve their goals.

3. To provide information, because being informed is 3/4 of the problem solved.

4. More accessible, funny, and enjoyable.

5. Care about people's needs first. No two clients are served the same way because they all have different needs or challenges.

6. Create and invent new ways of doing things to help other businesses make more money and get more customers.

7. Make sure to give much attention to my training participants. I do a lot of demonstrations and exercises with them and encourage them to practice together as often as possible. Between seminars, my

team contacts the participants to help them in their learning.

8. We created a much better way to sorting out equity-based opportunities in the startup space. Our "style" is very customer-centric. Everything is built out of customer interviews.

9. We took a mixture of what works great in the talent pool, user interfaces and backend optimizations to form a foundation for Intern Betas to grow.

10. I love experimenting (solo or with teams) to build solutions based on approaches that have worked in other industries.

11. I use existing business models to help me improve on mine since they have been at it longer than I have, and also to help explain the idea of what it's not, and what it's like. It's a skills incubator, not a boot-camp; it's closer to a learning circle and a hackathon having a baby.

12. The entire theme of the business is to exploit that overlap between punk counter-culture ethos (the art) and leading-edge software engineering (the science).

Your turn

MISSION

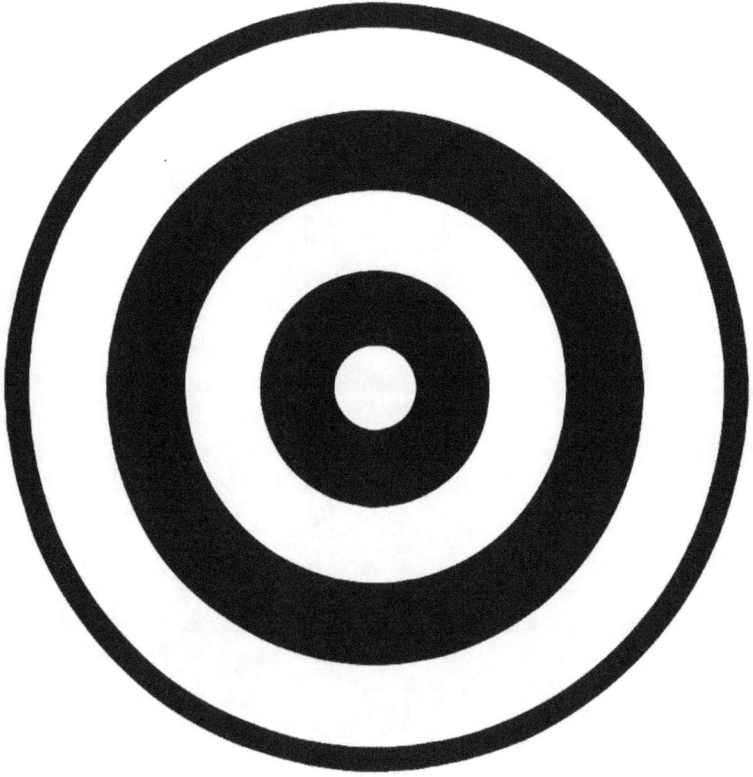

So you have found an idea and are ready to start your own business!

But why? Why you? Why your idea, your product? What is your mission?

   a) I don't know.
   b) I only want to make money.
   c) I want to become the best in the world, regardless of the field.
   d) I want to sell 100 000 copies of my product.
   e) I am born to succeed; this is my mission.
   f) I want to help people, everyone, anyone.
   g) None of the above.
   h) All of the above.

If your answer is H, I am speechless.

CTRL-E: Center

From idea to business, there is a long, long road.

The truth is: the sentence above contains two false premises that are, unfortunately, widespread.

1. "From idea to business": it is a mistake to think that it is "from idea to business". Rather, it is "from idea to customers." You should focus on customers and put the emphasis on them to create and improve your product. Don't be another self-centered entrepreneur who focuses on the business before the real needs of the target customers.

2. "There is a long, long road." First, here is the perfect road:

However, the first time you go down the road, it will look more like this:

The chances that you don't reach your destination are great. Not because the road is long, but because you are not centered on the right destination: the customers. This is the main cause of this sad statistic: nine out of ten companies close their doors during the first five years. And the one company that survives has only a 1 out of 10 chance of surviving the following five years.

A common mistake is to start by seeing this as a one-way road from idea to customers, and not the other way around.

Such a one-way road cannot lead anywhere but to a dead end into a bottomless pit.

The road from the idea to the customer's needs has traffic in both directions, allowing you to go back to the source (the idea) to improve it through feedback and testing, then validating or rejecting it quickly.

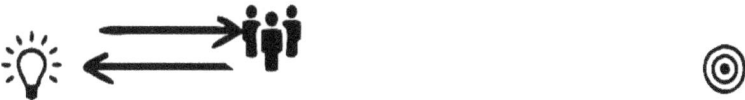

The beauty of this two-way road is that the more you go from your idea to customers and go back from customers to your idea, and so on, the smoother, shorter and less winding the road becomes.

Paradoxically, you will realize that the shorter the road is, the farther you will go. And believe me, you won't go alone. There will be more and more people accompanying you, without even knowing the destination, simply because we all like to participate in a project that is gaining momentum.

So, what is the destination?

Think of it as the mission you give yourself—the purpose of the project, by extension yours, and what motivates you to rush through the fog on the road.

Set your mission in one sentence:

_____

Writing down your mission in one sentence helps to prototype what we call the MVP, the Minimum Viable Product, and to get rid of any functionality or superfluous details that don't directly serve your mission.

For the target customers, this mission statement serves as a sales pitch. This one sentence differentiates you from your competitors and makes the customer buy first the idea, and then the product, or not buy anything.

The mission is also what keeps you focused on three essential pieces of luggage to bring with you on the road from the idea to the customers:

1. Your needs. First you must act accordingly to your wishes. It may sound selfish, but if you don't take care of yourself first, or if you don't respect yourself, how will you take care of your customers and their needs, which are similar to yours?

2. Customers' needs. Usually on one very specific need that you fill better than anyone else.

3. A single goal. In order not to scatter you and dilute your efforts, focus on one goal—one key metric. For example, the gross income or the number of online registrations, so you'll be able to determine quickly if your idea sticks to customers' needs or not.

It is too easy to be off-centered with so many attention-suckers in today's world. Among the many reasons why you can struggle staying focused, the principal reason remains: you don't listen to yourself. You'd rather listen to distortions of reality that are your beliefs, fears, principles, entourage and ideologies that cause a gap between who you are and who you want to be.

To ensure that you stay focused on your mission and have the motivation to reach your goal, try the following exercise:

Shrink the road as much as you can. The destination

being closer, how can you not see it?

Separate the road into small sections, each section representing a goal, a step. Place each step to act as a checkpoint, indicating that you are progressing in the right direction.

Once separated, look at the steps one by one again and judge their necessity. Be very critical; always doubt the relevance of them. If the step is not required, please get rid of it.

If it is indeed essential, ask yourself if it can be separated again to be divided into sub-steps and thus shorten the distance between each checkpoint even more.

Now name each step with the goal's name.

Now ask yourself how many checkpoints your project needs to hit the road and be viable. The fewer, the better. Often two or three checkpoints are enough: checkpoint #1, find the idea; checkpoint #2, call a friend; checkpoint #3, sell the idea and get paid, even before the product is created! The road from the idea to the customer is rather short from this perspective, right?

Of course, when your local employment center gives you its endless gameplan—business plan, business cards, website, training sessions—it's easier to get discouraged and fail than it is to stay focused on the three essential pieces of luggage:

1. Your needs

2. Customer's needs

3. A single goal

Next time anybody tries to fill your head with pre-made procedures, preconceptions or any other heavy/bogus/false stuff, say aloud these words, which are the precursors of all innovation: "What if...?"

My turn

I think we live in a time when staying centered and balanced has never been so hard. Everything tries to distract us, every time. Calls, emails, SMS, push notifications, social media, games, TV, the internet, porn.

We're one click away from anything and anyone. But, at the same time, we live in a time when starting a business has never been easier. Exactly because we're one click away from anything and anyone. Isn't it a beautiful paradox?

I live this paradox daily. I have so many things on my plate that it's painful and hard to stay at the center. That's one of the main reasons why I wrote this book. Every time I feel unbalanced, I step back, write or read a bit, focus, and go back to work. Every time I question myself about why do I do this or that, I refer to my mission, which is as relevant to this book as it is to my whole life: empower entrepreneurs to succeed and be happy.

Now you, what's your mission?

Their turn

Maybe you connect with the like-minded people who filled out my survey. Here are the top 20 missions I got:

1. Teaching and assisting realtors in the luxury market by defining their niche of competencies and providing a memorable experience for their customers.

2. To build relationships that last.

3. Do good work, for good people.

4. Deliver delightful experiences to everyone.

5. To be the nurse that everybody wants to have.

6. To help people feel better without pain and to help them be healthy.

7. To make a difference in people's lives, one presentation at a time.

8. To provide a good customer service. Most of the accountants are too busy, and they are not returning calls or emails. My mission is always to have time for them whatever the question.

9. To facilitate the exploration and development of the full potential of the human being as a whole through training, mentoring and a culture conducive to learning and mastering the capacities needed to

research and develop new tools and models in the field of communication.

10. To help entrepreneurs save more money.

11. To help people improve their lives so that they can change their world.

12. To build up capital (human, financial, and knowledge).

13. To build tools for each stage of a business, from idea to exit.

14. To leave a better world for my family.
15. To close the diversity gap in tech with skill, and the skills gap with diversity.

16. Growth, adoption, traction, repeat.

17. To maximize value for people we interact with.

18. To build a medium-sized progressive video game studio that produces memorable and unorthodox stories in video game form.

19. To help users understand how the very tiny, yet very powerful device in their pockets can make their lives so much better.

20. To create something that will go on to be larger than me.

Your turn

MVP
MINIMAL VIABLE PRODUCT

So, you know where you're going. But what is the first thing you'll do?

- a) I'll take a break to clear my head.
- b) I'll do my business plan.
- c) I'm going to make business cards.
- d) I'll hire someone to do my website and wait for customers to call me.
- e) I'm going to train and improve my skills in this area.
- f) I'll look on the Internet for what I should do.
- g) I need money. I'll go to the bank to take out a loan or re-mortgage my house.
- h) None of the above.
- i) All the above.

If you answered i, I'll probably cry.

Ctrl-F: Search

It is time to take action.

That means taking a step forward, then another, but it could also mean taking a step backward. Along the way, you will change many parts of your initial idea and all that you have done in the previous steps, and that's normal! Nothing is set in stone, and that's the whole point: to test and validate.

The exercise is to find your key elements, allowing you to launch your business and reach the first checkpoint as soon as possible, and the following.

That being said, what should you look for?

Too often, people are looking for money first before launching.

- I have to make a business plan, I need $50 000, I have to go to the bank, I need funding...

And then the project dies in the bud. Or they die crippled by debts.

To hear them, one would think that money is the end, not the means. An enthusiast who focuses on the distraction, which is money, instead of focusing on his project, loses focus of the three essential pieces of luggage and is off-centered.

So you might think money is the heart of a project. Try putting your heart first, and you will see that the money will come. The ultimate example is crowdfunding. A guy takes a camera, films his passion, submits his project on Kickstarter and voila! The money magically appears.

Otherwise, other people are looking for a store, an office, a co-founder, a mentor, subsidies, a continuous development training, help from the local business center. Those are the selfish people—selfish because they focus on the business's needs instead of the customers' needs. The customers don't need an office, or a co-founder, or a mentor, or training. What they want is for you to solve their needs and help them sleep at night.

Most government organisms, or other similar distractions, that are supposed to help you to launch your business make you forget that the road is not from idea to business, but from idea to customers.

Let's take the five previous shortcuts, Ctrl-A to Ctrl-E, where the initial emphasis was put on you and your idea. Using the same five shortcuts, let's now switch from "idea to business" to "from idea to customers" and really put the emphasis on customers, not on you or your idea or your business. Here's how the process to create a successful business should sound:

Ctrl-E: Stay focused.

Ctrl-D: On customers' needs with your unique Style.

Ctrl-C: Providing them an improved copy.

Ctrl-B: Of something that goes to the heart of their core, to meet their bold purpose.

Ctrl A: And improves the big PIC of their daily life.

"But where should I start?" You may ask.

Search first to bridge the riskiest element of your project. For most people and businesses, the single most risky element translates to their weaknesses. They seek to delegate their weaknesses to other people (or other companies) for whom these weaknesses are strengths.

Thus, they can remain focused on their strengths and spend more time in an activity where they are the only ones who are performing so brilliantly, and also where they create significant added value for the customer.

This principle of satisfying the riskiest element applies to any business, large and small, and differs depending on the nature of the business and the growth stage. For example, the riskiest element for a multinational company can be its partner in India to which it outsources manufacturing parts, while, for the small local garage, the riskiest element might be its revenue structure.

Still, regardless of the size and nature of the business, the riskiest element is almost always the same: the customers. This is even truer for a startup like yours. Will you get one customer, to begin with? Will there be a market? Can you make money out of it? Any simple questions you should ask yourself, as often as you brush your teeth, if necessary (I hope you brush them daily).

Too few people ask themselves these questions. They are too focused on their product or are too biased by other distractions that cause them to lose sight of the essential: human needs.

To validate if there is a customer and a need to fill, take this approach: sell first, and then worry about how you're going to handle the logistics and everything else needed to create the product that you sold. In short, get rid of everything else that sits between the idea and the customer and that could slow your pace. Shrink the gap between the two as much as you can and stay away from all distractions that separate you from each checkpoint.

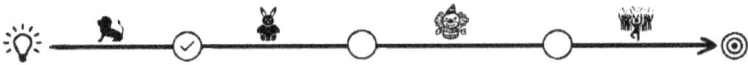

Your goal is to achieve the first checkpoint as soon as possible. Ask questions of all the people you meet along the way and validate with their feedback. Fast. Speed is the key to staying focused and motivated, propelling your project and carrying with it customers as well as employees, partners, and investors.

Once you reach the first checkpoint, to continue your journey towards the second one you will have to answer questions from the critics and listen to the feedback.

An error even more serious than the *off-centering* explained above is to strive for perfection. Everything that seems perfect to you is probably not perfect to your customers. For example, if you build an elephant and the customers want only the ivory, I guess you lost a lot of time and money.

Don't seek perfection. Try instead to achieve each checkpoint as fast as you can and give a damn good ride to customers!

My turn

The riskiest part of being a book author is to not get published. Trust me, that's a real pain in the ass. The first book I wrote never got published after months of waiting and negotiating with publishers. Basically, they said it was too new, too different and too risky. Isn't that the exact recipe of an awesome business opportunity?

Unfortunately, some authors become managers for publishing companies, without any clue about business—I can be hard on them, because they won't read this book anyway.

Fortunately, things have changed in the past 15 years, thanks to Lulu, CreateSpace and other self-publishing platforms. A simple Google of "self-publishing platform" saved me a lot of time and money. Why money? Because, far beyond the cliché that time is money, by using the crowdfunding method as the first step of my self-publishing strategy, I raised $5 000. A typical book author receives around 10% of royalty for each book sale. That means on a book sold for $20, the author gets $2. At this pace, I would have needed 2 500 sales to reach $5 000. Even if I were to sell five books a day, which is way far beyond my expectations, making 2 500 sales would still take 500 days.

I did it in 30 days.

That also solved the second riskiest element of this project: to get customers. After I had skipped the biggest and most feared risk by all authors—to not get published—I had no excuses...

If my book is bad, and no one buys it, I will know the truth at the moment it hits the market. Pre-launching it before these lines were written allowed me to find 110 backers and to sell around 150 copies. From there, only one very risky element remained: me, not writing the book.

Now you, what are you looking for, right now, to solve the riskiest part of your project?

Your turn

Ctrl-G: Go

Go.

The exercise is as simple as that.

You've searched for the riskiest element to satisfy it and to reach the first checkpoint. Well, do it now!

Go! Switch to drive mode.

You will notice that this is not as easy as it looks. It is even more difficult. And that's why so many aspiring entrepreneurs stop and give up here.

But not you.

Is your first checkpoint calling the marketing manager of Company X? Make the call! It takes 5 seconds to dial, 20 seconds to say nice words to the secretary, 30 seconds to make your pitch. In less than a minute, your first checkpoint is reached.

"One minute of discomfort that seemed like an eternity", you might say.

But oh so rewarding! Some people work eight hours a day, while you, in one minute, can accomplish more than them. And if that minute seems like an eternity, well, enjoy it—time is money. Imagine how much an eternity is worth!

In less than a minute, you can accomplish most of the work: validating if a customer and a need exist. Was the answer negative? Call the second marketing manager on your list and adjust your pitch, according to the valuable and relevant feedback from the previous manager. In short, refine your approach.

The one-minute phone call is just an example. Your first checkpoint can be anything, as long as it remains focused on the essential: the customer. Try different approaches and validate. Go!

You will see that, after each checkpoint you reach, your project gains momentum. Exponentially.

Repeat several times to reach several checkpoints, and do so as soon as possible. If running a business is a marathon, creating it is a sprint. In other words, the manager is a marathon runner. The entrepreneur is a sprinter.

And the latter will:

1. Go
2. As soon as possible
3. Repeat
4. Often
5. Take a different path
6. Refine his or her approach

?• ←——————————————→ !

Ctrl F   Ctrl G

Shortcuts Ctrl-F and Ctrl-G should constantly be iterating to find the answer to what will satisfy the riskiest elements, one by one.

$$? \longleftrightarrow !$$

ctrl F   ctrl G

To these fast, frequent iterations we must add the shortcut that closes the testing and validation loop, leading to the creation of your MVP:

Ctrl-H – Replace.

My turn

Like Nike or, more famously, Shia Lebeouf once said:

Here's what I did to get this book done:

1. First, I tested the concept on a few friends, talking about it as if it were already written, to see their real reaction.
2. I called five friends to help me get some answers about myself for shortcuts Ctrl-A and B.
3. I sent the first chapters to some random people.
4. I crowdsourced the content by creating a survey to get more real examples, to add some fresh meat to

the theory, whether because I'm a freak over efficiency or too lazy to do the research myself.

5. I hired a designer to help me with the book illustration, to create something nice for step #6 below.
6. I crowdfunded the cost of development by creating a Kickstarter campaign.
7. I sent the beta to the first backers, got a few feedbacks and one woman even completed the exercises of every shortcut, for real! I was blown away!
8. I spent a few days on marketing it (a few days, but a lot of hours!)
9. I created a website (actually more like a web page) in a few hours.
10. I emailed the backers to say I would be two months late—it's not because I write a book about business that I'm good at business. My bad.
11. I hired someone to proofread everything.
12. I created everything CreateSpace needs to be ready to sell my book as a hard copy and a digital copy on every device.
13. I said "Release the Kraken!" and unleashed the book.

Your turn

Ctrl-H: Replace

Let's go back a little to better move forward.

"Why change something, you might ask, as I'm trying to build my company at full speed? Would that not count as the mistake of seeking perfection?"

Not at all. The Ctrl-H shortcut completes the loop.

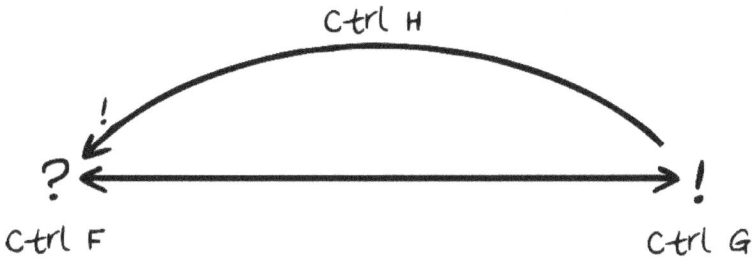

Let's recap. You have your MVP, which you offer to customers and that, at an infantile stage, must be flexible and malleable.

This is a bit like the newborn's skull, which allows the child to be released from its mother's womb. An image of Play-Doh is certainly more appealing.

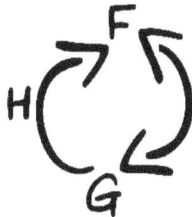

In the illustration below, we'll put a C for the Core at the heart of your business.

As you can see, the C looks like an ear. That's intended. It is to remind you that your customers are at the heart of your business, and you should always listen to them.

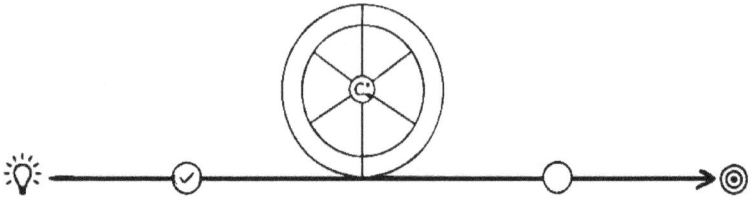

Around this core, you have the Style window, which you have defined thanks to the empathy wheel.

Over each customer interaction at every checkpoint you reach, you will reap the feedback that will shape the core of your business and validate it, as each layer around it, one by one.

How long should the core be malleable? As long as there is room for improvement and it creates an essential added value for the customer, in synergy with your company's mission defined in Ctrl-E. Actually, there is no deadline—but some people determine one to avoid falling prey to procrastination.

A company that only does Ctrl-F: Find and Ctrl-G: Go and never does Ctrl-H: Replace suffers very quickly from the worst of the incurable diseases: not adjusting to the changing needs of customers.

Ctrl-H is a shortcut that acts as a cure, relieving the performance of its weaker elements and eliminating any potential source of gangrene at the heart of your business.

Moreover, companies that keep a malleable core while growing, even the largest ones, or ones that create new cores when innovation does not fit the current core (we will discuss this concept later) are the only survivors.

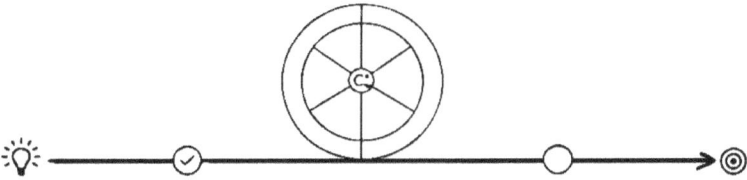

These three shortcuts could summarize how to develop your business every day.

Ctrl-F	→	Ctrl-G	→	Ctrl-H
Search		*Go*		*Replace*

Employee	Interview	Yourself
Customer	Networking event	Watching TV
Partner	Making calls	Current process
...	...	...

The same principle can be applied to any action or process for which you wish a continuous improvement, no matter the sphere of activity. Take examples from everyday life; you'll notice it's quite similar:

Ctrl-F ⟶ Ctrl-G ⟶ Ctrl-H
Search   *Go*   *Replace*

Wife	Dating site	Singleness
Health	Playing sports	Watching TV
Victory	Working out	Current process
...	...	...

Now list the results of your testing and validation period with target customers. Repeat as often and as quickly as possible to reach a level of sustained growth.

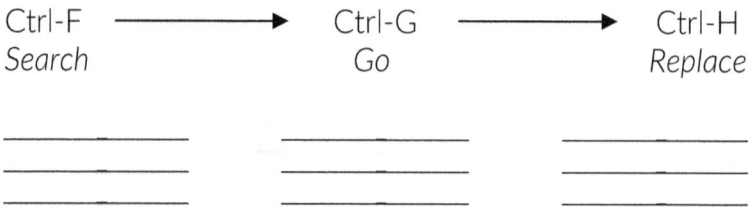

Ctrl-F ⟶ Ctrl-G ⟶ Ctrl-H
Search   *Go*   *Replace*

———————   ———————   ———————
———————   ———————   ———————
———————   ———————   ———————

Generally, two reasons lead us to Search ⟶ Go ⟶ Replace a part of the Core.

> 1. It does not work
> 2. Something more appropriate exists

These two reasons combine the force of an inevitable change that can be seen as creative destruction. This also applies to life as a couple!

My turn

Throughout the search and go process, I've replaced a lot of things. I started with my deepest and most intimate thoughts and fears.

I've also replaced:

- The traditional book publisher by CreateSpace.
- The designer I had for another one, better, cheaper.
- The title (the original title was SSSH! - Secrets Shortcuts to Success & Happiness).
- The cover design (five or six times, maybe more—I'm a freak).
- Working on client's projects, to take time to write this book.
- My face in the Kickstarter video, for the one of a cute 6-year-old boy smarter than me.

And you, what did/do/will you replace to make it work?

Their turn — CTRL F-G-H

Here are the top 20 answers I got in my survey to the questions: "From idea to market, what is your usual path? How do you find what to create? How do you validate? How do you know when you should replace/change something?"

1. When I started my business, I validated the business model by interacting with realtors in a networking cell and by asking them what is their main problem with their business. Their answer was quite simple and defined the main focus of my business: innovative marketing strategies for realtors.

2. It's easy. Ask someone what he doesn't like and by his answer, he will give you ideas.

3. I begin by researching the domain I am working within. To whom am I trying to appeal? What am I trying to accomplish? What are my limitations? And this last question is perhaps one of the most important because limitations are really what spur the most creativity. You have to draw a box around yourself to really be able to create outside of it.

4. A long time ago, someone told me a fun way to explore ideas. Ideas are cheap; they're like $1. When you draw an idea out, it costs you $10. When you design an idea out, it's $100. When you code an idea out for testing, it's $1 000. The key is staying in the first two buckets because it's the cheapest and the most flexible way to find what you need.

5. I listen to questions people ask.

6. What to create usually comes from a number of questions I get on a specific topic, or a number of visitors for specific articles on my blog. Validation is done by asking some contacts to review and comment what I did. And I know it's time to replace or change when trends seem to change in my trade readings.

7. I always take an idea and twist it into a new idea. Creating something new is the way to stand out and make people notice you.

8. If my clients recommend me as a tax person, that means I'm on the right track. If I do something wrong, I'll know from them, and I'll adjust myself.

9. Generally, my training development ideas come from findings that I make when clients come to see me in coaching consultations. I test my ideas during the consultations or existing formations. When the reactions are positive, I adopt these new ideas and develop the topic more deeply!

10. Validate with a landing page. Get enough signups to start the interview. Release quick and dirty MVP. Test. Get feedback. Iterate. When people are ripping your product out of your hands, you have PMF (product market fit). "Run, Forrest, Run!"

11. Partner up, release early, test and understand, nail it and then scale it.

12. Creating tools like naked investing, social contracts with mentors and diagnostics for export readiness.

13. Creating methods like roots2fruits and export accelerators.

14. Talk to customers and constantly iterate.

15. Better discussed over a beer, Just Do It. It's about fulfilling needs.

16. I'm in validation phase, not to market yet. I change something when an idea I had gets invalidated and replaced by an actual need, or when I learn about some existing behavior from clients that I can tap into.

17. Being detailed, observe, and anticipate based on history.

18. Number of people clicking.

19. Our staff throws out ideas regularly just conversationally. Sometimes they're jokes and sometimes they elicit a different response, a more serious tone. Those are the ones we explore deeper, talk about and discuss how they might behave in video game form. Are they stories worth telling? Is there an audience who would want to experience that? We don't make stories just for us; we want to make video game stories for an audience that would love to explore that world in a new medium. We begin prototyping with a small team, and the project will either die at conception due to several important 'gates', or it will flow on and start to become something amazing. When it doesn't play well, or the team is losing interest or momentum we pay attention to whether that's because the game isn't as exciting as we might have imagined or because they're simply having an unproductive day. If it's the former, we re-assess.

20. My unusual path to my project came from observing my "tribe" over a number of years. Seeing how others were dealing with the same issues, then researching the options to help, lead me to kick off what I need to do. Validation came from a survey sent to members of the community I was seeking to help. I know I need to replace the current options because they are currently too expensive for the current market and don't offer a good user experience.

Your turn

BUSINESS MODEL

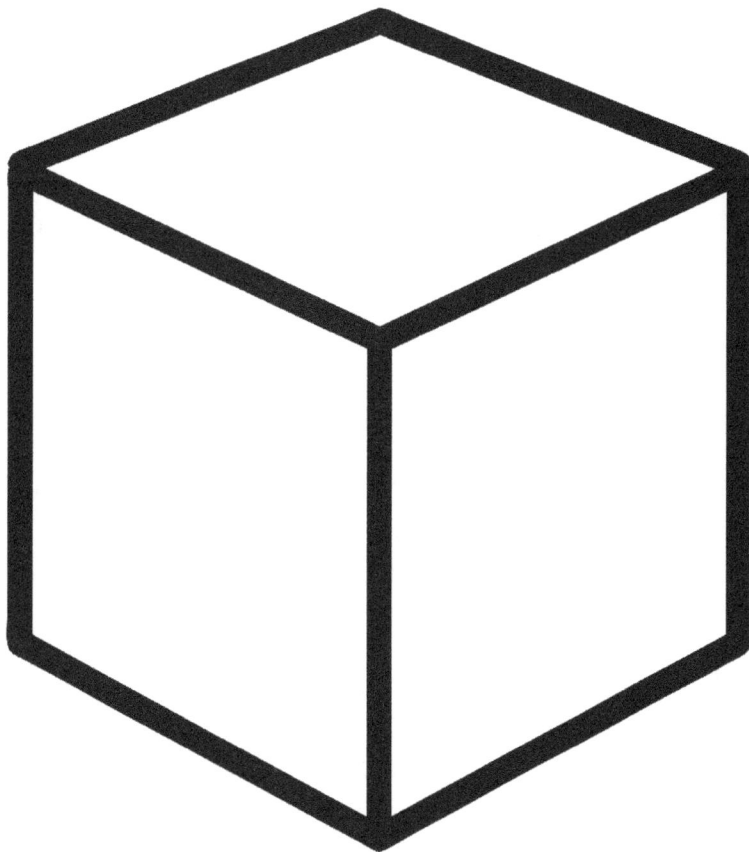

So you tested and validated your product and found out what works. What is it? On what should you focus? Will you make money out of it? How much? Where can you find the most revenues and the lowest costs?

In short, what's your business model?

a) What's that?
b) I don't know.
c) I'm not a capitalist.
d) I don't want to make money; I do it for fun.
e) I'll find out later.
f) Facebook lost money for years, so why should I care about that?
g) None of the above.
h) All of the above.

If your answer is F, you better have a damn good idea and an even better team! You will need a killer idea and a truckload of luck to find people that believe so much in you and your idea that they're willing to lose millions each year.

If your answer is G, you're on the right track. Turn the page.

Ctrl-I: *Italic*

You have come a long way so far. Search. Go. Replace. Search. Go. Replace...

You have probably tried several things and taken several paths to reach your checkpoints.

The exercise to do now: focus on what worked.

This exercise is actually to *italicize*—which means to emphasize, as it's the most popular use of italics—two aspects: the minimum viable product (MVP) and the business itself.

First, let's *italicize the MVP*.

You've tried things that have not worked (which is normal), and you've also tried things that worked well.

Keep the good ones in your company's core by referring to concrete evidence of success: what you've experimented, what you've seen on the street, real-life use cases, customers' testimonies, what people were willing to pay for...

You can go even further by referring to more advanced statistics, but the most important is to collect examples and details of each *meeting* between the customer and your product. Something like:

_____
(customer's name)

needed _____
(customer's need)

and liked _____
(feature, aspect or use)

because _____
(customer's main reason).

Creating these narratives will serve you in six ways. It will:

1. Inspire other people to buy and, importantly, use your product. It is essential to differentiate the verbs _buy_ and _use_: the first one gives you a sale; the second one, more than three sales.

2. Give new application ideas. That is to say, use your product in a different way than you imagined initially.

3. Make you discover a different customer segment.

4. Inspire the trust of customers, employees, partners and investors, especially the most suspicious, in your business.

5. Build storytelling around the company. Give gas to word-of-mouth.

6. Sell. And sell more. Because everything leads back to sales, which is your company's engine.

Focusing on concrete examples will help you justify, supported by numbers, the relevance of your product in the market, which will attract new customers, partners, employees and investors.

These people will need concrete facts and simplicity to get on board. For simplicity, I refer to the fact that people usually only read the headlines in the newspapers and nothing more, so your "concrete" must be summarized in a newspaper headline!

In this regard, Daniel H. Pink explains six simple ways to sell through headlines that he describes as six successors to the elevator pitches. Do the exercise. Describe your MVP, or what you sell, in a matter of:

- 1 word
- 1 question
- 1 rhyme
- 1 email subject line
- 1 tweet
- 1 Pixar story summary: *Once upon a time there was _____. Every day, _____. One day _____. Because of that, _____. Because of that, _____. Until finally _____.*

What you sell must be simple—hence the importance of avoiding too much innovation and creating an enhanced copy of something known by people that works well. What you sell should also be out of the ordinary—read extraordinary—to get people to talk about it and spread the word. So, something simple and extraordinary. Don't think because a product is simple that it's necessarily boring!

"Simplicity is the ultimate sophistication", once said Leonardo da Vinci.

This principle should apply to any action you do, not only at the MVP stage.

In the same vein, the principle of *italicizing* should not only apply to your product but also the business itself.

The goal here is to build a successful business model with an emphasis on the best customers, the best employees and partners, the best activities and especially on the best revenues and—this could sound strange—on the best expenses, the vital ones and the ones with the best ROI.

Suppose you make a film about your life, while you live it—which is the very principle of reality TV shows—and that before every action, you ask yourself: "What do I want to see on the screen for the moment I am about to live?"

It may seem extreme and narcissistic but do it. You'll see, it helps. See your business adventure as a good action movie. See each checkpoint as the scene where you fight the bad guy. And remember that the more checkpoints you have, the more adventures you have and the faster they are fought and won, the better the action movie is!

Got an accident? It doesn't matter; it's just a movie! Unable to defeat the bloodthirsty villain at the end? Fight harder! He beats you every time? Cease to struggle alone and *italicize* on finding allies: customers, employees, partners, investors and cash flow.

Your MVP has attracted an army of people ready to fight by your side; you would be foolish not to use them to destroy the nasty end-game monster!

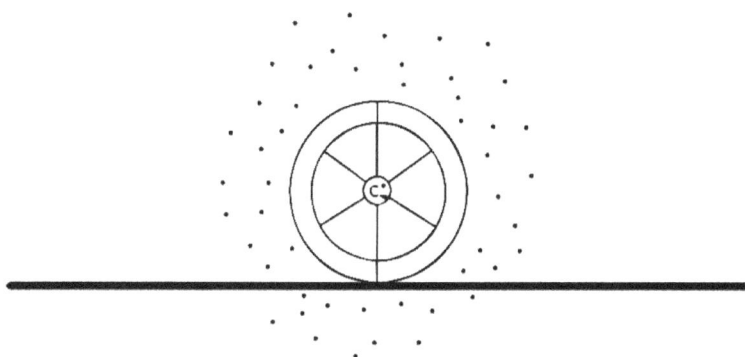

P.S. Remember, the only person who can make the film boring is you. And the worst evil monster, the one who always puts himself through your road and tries to block you in every possible way, is you again. Once you realize that, nothing and nobody can stop you.

My turn

Among everything that I tested and tweaked until now, I decided to *italicize* on what enticed people at first and what I never changed: the keyboard shortcuts analogy.

In cinema, we call a movie that sells in one punchy sentence a "high concept" movie.

"It's the story of a guy that is born old and become young with time." Which movie this is?

Benjamin Button has a very powerful concept. It's catchy and it sells itself. If you forget the title of this movie but remember that it's the story of an old man who becomes younger, you will find *Benjamin Button* in seconds by googling it. It's the same thing with most of the very successful movies—good or not, remember *Aliens vs. Cowboys*?

I want to do the same with my book. This helps ensure that the next time you hear "Hey, do you know the book about some keyboard shortcuts to success", you will spread the word.

Far beyond that, I want to create the same psychological effect that makes a dog come when he hears a bell. I'm not saying you're an animal; what I'm saying is that maybe, next time you are on your computer and press Ctrl-C to copy something and then Ctrl-V to paste it, you will remember this book and the lessons you've learned. Maybe it will motivate you to work harder—who knows!

To conclude, I want to clarify two things:

1. I italicized the high concept for my book, but a book is not a typical business. That being said, most of the time you will put the emphasis somewhere else.
2. You can italicize more than one thing, but don't pick too many things. At this stage, your business can't be that different and unique; I mean, to innovate that much and that fast on more than one aspect of a business is pretty risky and is usually a bad decision. Stay focused on what really differentiates your business—don't re-invent the wheel.

Your turn now: what should you *italicize?*

Your turn

Ctrl-J: Justify

What's your purpose?

If you haven't found it yet, go back to Ctrl-A and repeat the exercises until Ctrl-E.

These shortcuts are intended to help you discover your big PIC (Ctrl-A) and focus on your bold purpose (Ctrl-B) to create an improved copy (Ctrl-C) of something that meets customers' needs (Ctrl-D), which will allow you to thrive and stay centered on your mission (Ctrl-E).

You can use the same logic to articulate your business purpose.

You must find and justify its raison d'etre—its purpose in the eyes of customers, but also its purpose for you.

How many people create an ephemeral business just to work for themselves, like wannabe entrepreneurs?

- I went into business! A construction company!
- Oh yeah?! And what's the difference between you and the neighbor?
- My prices are competitive!
- Stop it, you'll make me cry.

Or

- Did I tell you I'm now a financial advisor?
- Really?! And how different are you from the other three guys who approached me this

month to manage my portfolio?
- I give personalized service!
- Oh, I see...

By "justify its purpose", I mean differentiating from others by improving the life of a small group of people—your life, first. With time, sweat and luck, make a small difference in the world, your way.

In Ctrl-I, you've put the emphasis on what works from the Ctrl-F-G-H loop.

The time has come to find the meaning of all the information gathered. To deepen, to document, to realign the whole thing. In short, to justify.

Clarify and purify what you offer, so you are prepared for the official launch of your product. As if you were invited to the prom, put on your best clothes. This advice applies to your product as well as for you, because you're about to meet the essential contacts to grow your project quickly.

Customers: Justify by other customers' testimonials
Team: Justify by inspiration, mission and numbers
Value proposition: Justify by sales
Activities: Justify by the need and productivity
Revenue: Justify by the quality and quantity
Costs: Justify by the ROI

Don't waste six months to build a business plan, find an office, take a refresher course or any other limiting beliefs. Just build a business model that will provide real results.

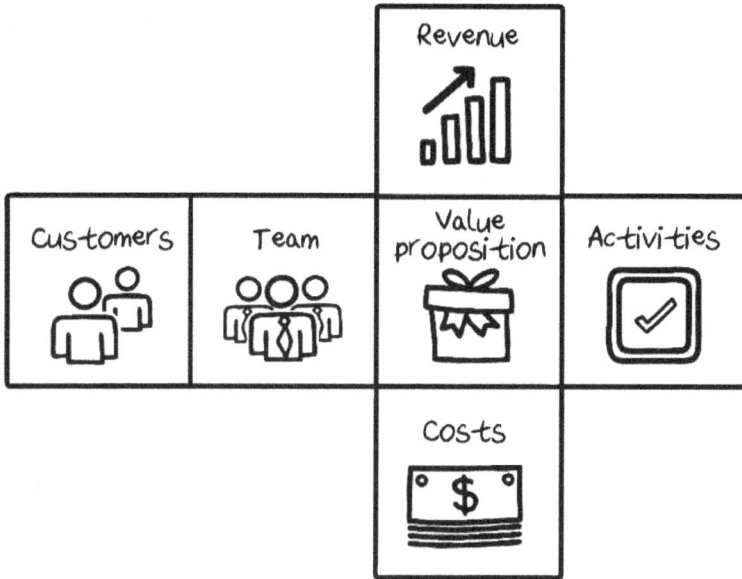

Let's face the truth: until now, you've only had a minimal viable product, not a business. The exercise to create your business model and justify every part of it will transform you from a product owner to a business owner.

In the cube template below, write down, in each square frame, in as few words as possible, what the core of your business is that justifies the existence of your company.

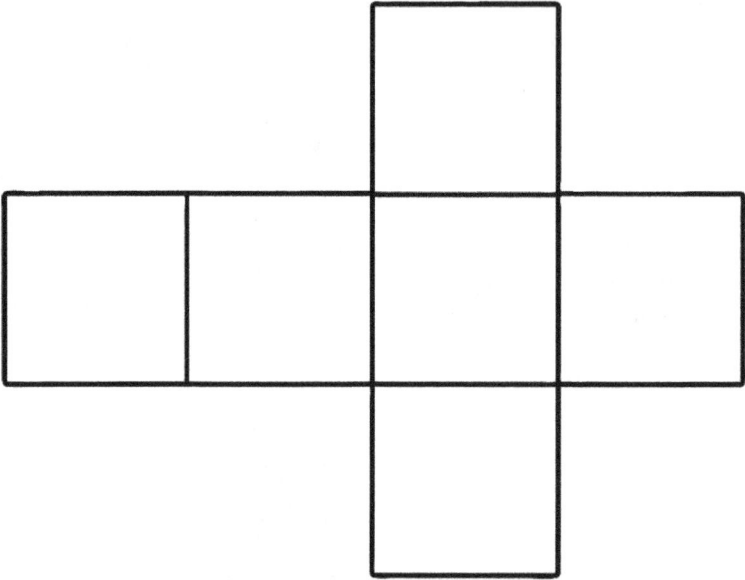

Go further than that. Justify the relevance of your daily actions that make your business grow. Get rid of the rest, at least from your core business, or change the way you do things. For example, delegate instead of doing yourself.

Once this is done, get ready to officially launch your business and build key relationships with a bunch of people who will be impressed by your best prom clothes.

My turn

My experience until now justified some of my hypotheses about the book itself. And that's the whole point of all the previous shortcuts. I could then consider that I have my MVP.

I know the high concept sells by itself. The Kickstarter campaign proved it. Are we done? You must be kidding— we're just beginning!

I don't know a lot about the book industry, but I know that 95% of the authors are starving. And that's even closer to 100% if they rely only on their books to make money. The 5% of authors who make money use their books as a business card, as a tool to make something else that is more lucrative: conferences, workshops, consulting, name it.

I'll have to do the same if I want to create a business out of it. But that could come down the road, from the moment the book gets traction. If I, like too many people that launch too many things at once, focus on creating conferences, workshops, consulting, and my book is shitty or is known only by my parents because I'm too busy creating my conferences that nobody will attend because the book is shitty or because they don't know it, I'm fucked.

This may look like a funny example, but I hear much funnier ones daily.

So I'll focus on the core business first, because of the reason above and also because I don't want to confuse myself and my customers with too much stuff. And by the way, I don't believe a great author can also pretend to be a great speaker as well as a great teacher. A great speaker gives a show to his audience. A great teacher is more methodic than charismatic. And a great author writes a book in his basement with no window. Anyway, here's a sketch of how I justify my business model, for now. I'll let you, dear customer, tell me what you want and what I should do next.

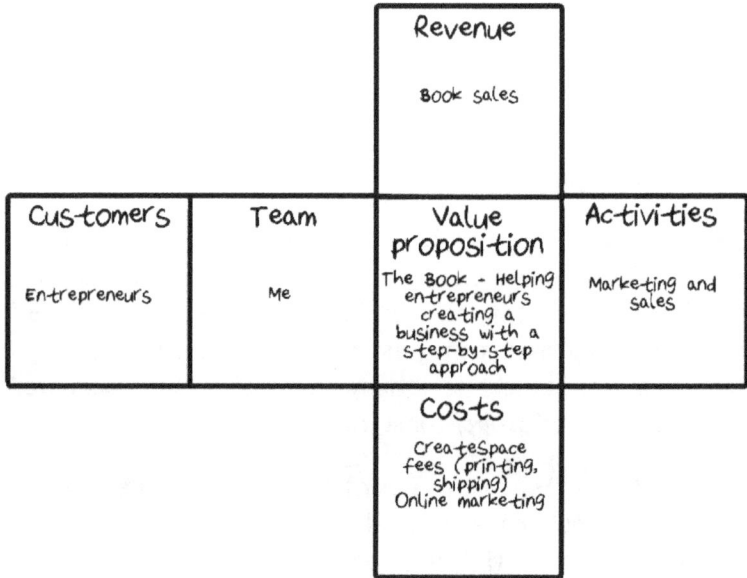

		Revenue Book sales	
Customers Entrepreneurs	**Team** Me	**Value proposition** The Book - Helping entrepreneurs creating a business with a step-by-step approach	**Activities** Marketing and sales
		Costs CreateSpace fees (printing, shipping) Online marketing	

Their turn – CTRL I-J

Here are the top 7 answers I got in my survey to the question: "What's your business model?"

1. When I meet prospects, I give them a perfect example and some testimonials of the implementation of my marketing strategies in the luxury real estate market. I am not only teaching how to improve their marketing creatively, but I am also implementing the strategies with them. And, to top things off, I am open to financing their deals!

2. Personal training, group training, conferences, rehabilitation and prevention.

3. My business model is simply to create a human environment solution in which professionals from all spheres of activities can learn, master, and contribute to the development of approaches, tools and applications in their respective fields. To achieve this, we organize training courses and seminars in our training room. One of my advantages is to have a strong team of trainers that I myself have formed.

4. A monthly membership for access to the network.

5. We have 3 business models: first we do consulting as presales to validate needs and markets (fee for service); second, we invest in teams and ventures that can develop and deliver solutions to ventures and ecosystems; third, we contribute ~25% of net profits back to those who cannot afford tools as part of social enterprise mission.

6. Video games are a hit-based business, and there are many ways to approach building a studio. Our approach is to apply years of experience on triple-A titles, a source of seed capital and a strong IP to something original and high quality out of the gates. It's bold, it's risky, but the payoffs match that risk. If it doesn't work, you can always contract the studio to build a game for someone else while you lick your wounds and plan your next try.

7. My model is pretty simple; revenue stream #1 comes from app downloads, #2 in-app sales, #3 offering third-party SaaS for targeted retailers.

Your turn now: how do you justify your current business?

Your turn

GROWTH

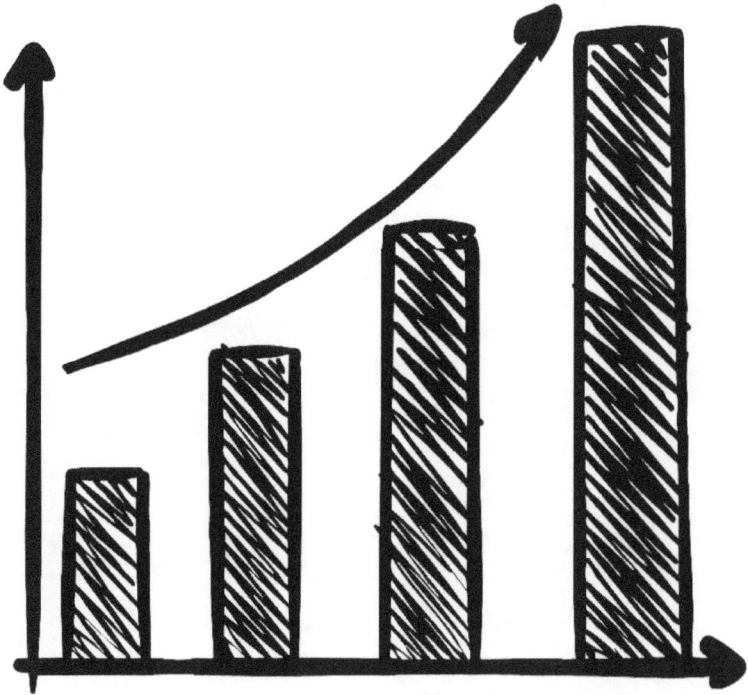

So, you've put the emphasis on what works and built a business model with a high growth potential. But how can you transform this potential into real growth?

a) I'll wait for people to come.
b) I think word of mouth will spread.
c) I'll subscribe to the chamber of commerce.
d) Growth? I don't want that; I want to keep my thing small.
e) What is a business model?
f) I'll hire an expensive marketing agency.
g) I'll ask my mom what she thinks.
h) All of the above.
i) None of the above.

What else to say other than turn the page?

Ctrl-K: Hyperlinks

Hyperlinks. That sums up the art of doing business.

For most people, I mean *normal* people, the difference between a link and a hyperlink is simply summarized by the prefix *hyper*. But what is it exactly, beyond its linguistic definition? What does it mean for an entrepreneur like you, who doesn't want to settle for a simplistic conclusion reached by people who don't pursue the mission you pursue every single day?

A hyperlink is a person to whom you have access in one click, one call or one action and who really helps you.

Think of a "big shot" you admire and think about how easy it seems for him or her to move a mountain in a single phone call. The reason is simple: that person is full of hyperlinks.

To grow your business, you need to quickly grow your network of contacts and create and maintain your hyperlinks. At this stage where you are, it's all about whom you know, who knows you, whom you know who knows someone, and who knows you through someone else.

Not only the number but also the quality of hyperlinks around you will be the determining factor in your journey's success. Real life works exactly like Google's search engine: more and better hyperlinks equal better rankings.

From this perspective, the difference between a link and a hyperlink, sometimes thin and difficult to predict, returns to the difference between failure and success. This is why the most experienced entrepreneurs are unanimous on this point: one of the most important mistakes that a young entrepreneur makes is starting a business without first taking the time to build his or her network.

How many successful startups have a single founder? How many successful ideas have been validated by one person alone before getting traction? Who will buy a product that even your closest friends don't care about? How many people will know about your product the day you launch? How can you alone support the cash flow needed to grow (I hope your dad is rich)? Who won't let you down during bad times (I hope you have an entrepreneurial spouse with a ton of empathy)?

If you create hyperlinks and take care of them, whether you're selling life insurance today and toothbrushes 10 years from now, your contacts will follow you and will be your first buyers and your best salespeople, or even your future employees! In short, they will drive your professional success and thereby your personal happiness.

What if your contacts don't buy? At least they will listen to you. This is a rare commodity that has as much if not more value in this hyper-stimulated world where attention is the new currency, and where time is more expensive than money. In this environment, you can save a lot of time and money by using your hyperlinks to quickly create a lot of added value.

According to Wikipedia (from which I replace the word *"anything"* with *"someone"*), a hyperlink allows you to:

1. Refer to *someone* who has already proven his or her credibility in this area.

2. Trust *someone*. Delegate your weaknesses to those people for whom they are strengths.

3. Focus on creating added value, not on rewriting what has already been said by *someone* else.

4. Be up-to-date thanks to his or her dynamism. You can change the content, but the link remains the same. It evolves with the two persons it bonds.

5. Create a web of people with specific skills.

6. Share affinities.

Let's go. Build your web. Insert hyperlinks, right in the heart of people, your customers, your team... In short, create a tribe around your business.

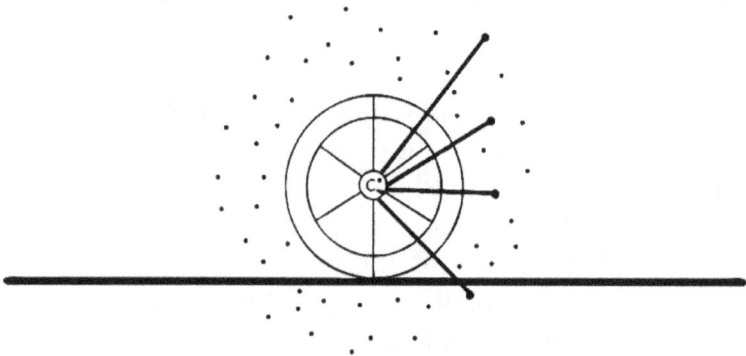

My turn

Who can help me grow my business? Who can make me go from a craft to a real business, which is by definition something I can make a living from?

Some call them key influencers. I like to call them hyperlinks because they open a new window of opportunity in a single click.

In every stage of growth, you will meet dead-links and hyperlinks. What's tricky is that as long as you don't click, you don't know which is which, who is who.

Let me give you a tip I've learned the hard way since I started my business: there are a lot more dead-links than hyperlinks—and most of them don't have a funny 404 page that makes you stop swearing (nerd joke).

Another tip. Like the dessert you don't want because you say you're too full until you know it's included, you should take it—it's free. Stop focusing on partnerships. Focus on sales.

Partnerships will make you feel better, at best, giving you the impression you had a busy day closing a big deal. But at the end of the day, your sales will be the same. The reason is simple: your new partner, like you, has nothing to offer but all to take. There are two sellers, and there is no buyer in the room. What do you expect?

Let me give you an example of how I quickly escaped from a *potential* partnership and turned it into a sale. A friend of mine, a best-selling author, told me she would help me sell more books. She generously suggested selling my book next to hers at her events.

- Give me $5 per book, she said.
- You should make more money, I replied... Let's do a deal. You buy 100 books from me for $1 200, so $12 each, and you sell them for $20 apiece, which is less expensive than on Amazon, so people will buy them right there and not lurk and buy later online. And you make $8 per book, which is 60% more than $5.

Am I crazy or just a really bad businessman?

Maybe.

She accepted.

That relieved me from any risk and gave me a $1 000 cash flow—the most valuable asset of every business.

Your turn

Ctrl-L: Align left

Were you always told to take your time to get it right?

Well... People around you have always lied and didn't want you to succeed!

To take your time is the best way to fail, to do things wrong, to not complete a task, or worse, to never take action.

Don't take your time. Accelerate! Because:

1. You will carry 80% of the results with 20% of the effort.

2. The remaining 20% of the results will be accomplished through hyperlinks created in Ctrl-K.

3. Parkinson's law proves that work expands to fill the time available for its completion. That means you will perform a task in the time allocated to complete it, no matter how much time is allocated.

4. Fixed deadlines and smaller time frames—see Timeboxing—will help you focus on the most important things, reduce risk and deliver a smaller scope faster.

5. In addition to #3 and #4 above, the Pomodoro Technique preaches that quick sprints combined

with high focus, with frequent and short breaks that will improve your mental agility, is the best way to successfully complete a great project.

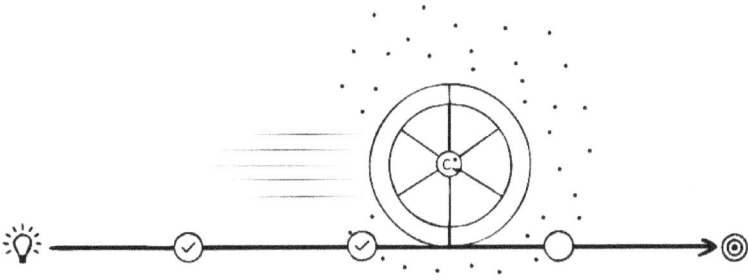

Your success is equivalent to a marathon of small sprints to reach checkpoints.

In Ctrl-K, you contacted hyperlinks, people you know who can be reached in a single click and who open a new window of opportunity. Some of them will propel you to the next level; some of them will not, maybe because they turned out to dead-links over time or just because their growth potential will never materialize.

But how will you know which of those hyperlinks will bring high growth? How will you recognize them?

Simple. The ones located in front of you.

- In front of me? People blocking me?
- Not at all. People you meet on your way, going faster than you and pulling you forward.

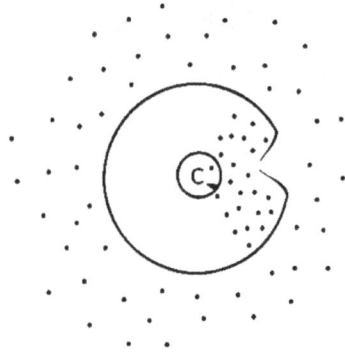

You can quickly identify a handful of hyperlinks that can get you to a whole new level. Create space for these people inside your company. Give them some room to express their mastery!

It is crucial to have these people on board to grow and prepare to go into fifth gear. These people are commonly called The Accelerators, the opposite of those who will only slow you down: The Piano Men.

Piano Men   Accelerators

   vs

Only one type will help you succeed and reach the next checkpoint. Guess who?

To get Accelerators on board, you must make room, get rid of trivia, do spring cleaning, give shares...

No matter. They should enter. Here is the maneuver.

Remember first to have:

Ctrl-I: Put the emphasis on what works.
Ctrl-J: Justified to attract and entice the key elements.
Ctrl-K: Created hyperlinks.

Now you need to align yourself left at the pilot position, to make room in the passenger seat for the Accelerators: your right arms.

Note that you are the pilot, so listen to the Accelerators but stay firm and decisive. You are the leader.

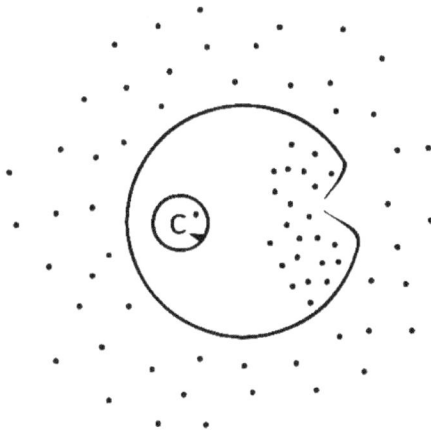

This is the stage where you start seeing more and more traffic (competitors) on the road because your business is growing, propelled by your drive and the Accelerators' fuel.

When you think of aligning left, what's the first thing you think, intuitively? Overtaking on the highway. Well, do it! Line up left and pass!

- They are so slow in the right lane!
- Exceed them on the left!

It is time for accelerated execution... must be blazing fast!

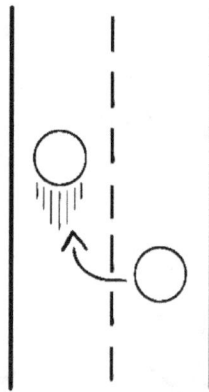

- Congratulations! Go to the next step and reap $200! Or $400, $1 000, $10 000 or more; it depends on the size of your market and the speed at which you drive!

Finally, here are some tips about what NOT to do:

- Observe speed limits and all the road signs.

- Fear accidents. Go to hell, accidents! You'll get into some, and that's great! They will make you a better driver! Getting into accidents illustrates that you take risks and that you are aggressive. This is excellent!

- Indicate your intent to overtake another business by putting on the flashing lights. Since when are competitors calling to tell they will crush you?

- Look back to see if a competitor is beyond you.

- Check your blind spots.

In short, don't apply what you were taught in driving school. Create your own rules.

My turn

The more you speed up, the more you meet Accelerators.

As my crowdfunding campaign got a bit of traction, I got a few Accelerators—who actually are often people you don't expect or people you don't know, like 75% of all the people who backed my campaign.

I got a crazy insight to offer a $1 000 reward for my Kickstarter campaign, which was: *You (and your startup) as the main character of the story. I always dreamt of being a superhero, so I offer you this chance!*

Honestly, this was kind of a joke. I mean the book's first draft was almost done, and there still wasn't a main character in the story, except for the intro. And then, at 2:46 pm on a beautiful Wednesday of July, a guy I didn't know—no common friends on Facebook, imagine—brought the $1 000 reward.

The guy's name is Eric Lafontaine, owner of EL Alliance. I searched for him all day long. Then I found him, and our first Facebook conversation went something like:

Me: Why the hell did you give me $1 000? It's too much, man!
Him: I think we Quebecers don't support each other enough.
Me: Wow, thanks man. You helped me a lot. I mean, that's a huge gift!
Him: Wait until you sell 10 000 copies—maybe my gift will be a pretty good investment, after all!

If you want to know more about Eric's story, I share it throughout the book, as the first story of each "Their turn" section.

A couple of days later, my girlfriend invited his partner Walid to eat at our home. We barely spoke about my book— I'm an author, it's easier for me to write than to speak. The day after, when I woke up, I had a push notification from the Kickstarter app saying that someone had bought 25 copies of my book for $500 while I was sleeping. I always told myself that was because my girlfriend is a damn great chef!

As I progressed at high speed on the highway to launch, I met a lot of great people in a very short period of time. The initial traction of my project made people want to jump on board. I would have thought more people would be jealous or simply wouldn't support me because it's only me, and I can't be a great author. I guess I was wrong. Or maybe I was going so fast that I didn't see them stuck down the road, out of gas.

I got proposals to guest post on popular blogs like the biggest French Canadian business blog and the biggest job site in Quebec. I presented a webinar to a business lecture club. I recorded a podcast for the Lifestyle University and so on. All that brought traffic and drove sales.

Accelerators gave me a boost to reach my milestones faster. But, more than everything, they gave me a boost of confidence.

Their turn — CTRL K-L

Here are the top 15 answers I got in my survey to the question: "What's your growth strategy?"

1. I am constantly networking to grow my network of contacts: cocktails, breakfasts, cruises, etc. I never hesitate to make good use of it. In order to move my business forward faster, I am aligning myself with strong business people with proven track records.

2. My strategy is to find partners to complete me. I can't do everything as a freelancer. So I try to find a designer and programmer that fit with me and my objectives. When we work as a team, we are 200% more efficient and the clients get a better result, and the product is built faster.

3. A small ball, like a baseball, focuses on who's out in the field right now. Find people who use your product so much they might kill you if you stripped it from them. Understand what are the "a-ha" moments they have when using your product. Find out if there are 100x people like them in the world, or if you can modify your product slightly to reach 100x the people. Run like the wind if you find it.

4. Adwords with Google, Facebook, word of mouth.

5. Group training, free conferences, networking.

6. Giving access to more content online. Surrounding myself with great partners to improve my online presence/strategy is key to improving my growth.

7. Our growth strategies: 1) Do as much public speaking as possible. 2) Get out and make friends with your competitors and pick their brains. 3) Never stop learning, because the more we know, the more valuable we can be to our market. 4) Always add to our company with new employees/consultants to improve our value proposition to our clients, which increases revenue and upsells results.

8. I'm very engaged in my communities. I'm living and working here. I'm on the board of directors at a gymnastic club, I'm a part of a mentoring program, I'm implicated in an economic summit. I'm in two networking groups. That being said, the more you are involved, the more people know you, and then more business comes in. Plus, I have a website, a Facebook page and an Instagram account.

9. Create many affiliate links with other companies working in the same field, but especially train and certify many trainers who themselves will create their own training schools in NLP, hypnosis, coaching and related areas, and who will hire me or members of my team, to provide training to their own original students in the future.

10. Serve customers better and ask for references.

11. We are driving a lot of organic traffic from Twitter and Quora. And Facebook ads work very well. We are also applying to 500 Startups. I have close ties with mentors there that I developed by placing second at Google's Startup Next in LA.

12. Pareto's law applies: 80% comes from 20%.

13. We invest in people through mentoring, skill training, and projects. We are then able to help align them with opportunities that align with their passion/purpose.

14. Finding and retaining advisors within our field who can expedite growth.

15. I've tried to be honest and transparent in all my dealings. To tell the team exactly where we are, why we are, and even open ourselves to their input when times are tough. That's paid off in countless ways. Word spreads that we treat our employees like adults, like little entrepreneurs, and the result of that is people saying things like "this is the most amazing place I've ever worked." Though maximizing profits is always nice, it's secondary to maximizing the health, happiness and welfare of our creative team.

Now you: what can drive you at high speed, high growth?

Your turn

PROFIT

So, you have created hyperlinks and accelerated. But how will all of this turn into profits?

a) I'll leverage my business on my hyperlinks and on their businesses.
b) I'll ask them to introduce me to their hyperlinks.
c) I'll keep on going at lightning speed.
d) I'll work my ass off and hustle to make this business worth millions.
e) I'll focus my time where it pays off the most.
f) I'll increase the most profitable activities and decrease the most expensive.
g) I'll try to reduce my costs as much as I can.
h) All of the above.
i) None of the above.

I'm sure you answered H.

Ctrl-M: Margins

- You should reduce your margins.
- Really? Why? Are you nuts?
- Maybe... I mean I started a business, after all, this is how people see me...
- No, I mean why reduce margins? The only way to make real money is to increase margins on every product sold!
- You're right. But I'm referring to something else. Have you ever been driving at breakneck speed?
- Maybe once.
- Well at this speed, the slightest detail can cause your loss.
- What's your point?
- To reduce the margin. To get rid of unnecessary things inside your business, which can only delay the achievement of achieving your mission.
- Got it!

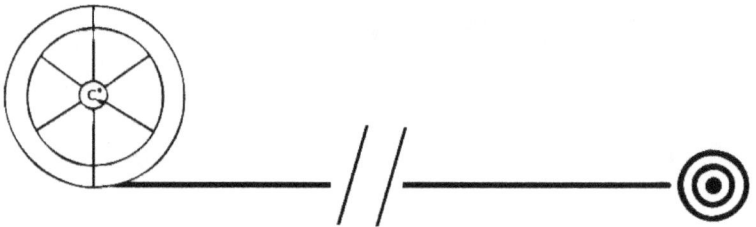

- I'm not sure you do.
- C'mon, stop acting like a philosopher!
- There are two main margins to reduce.
- Let me guess: the margin between me and my goal?
- Exactly! The margin between your business's

current position and your main goal. Man, you're smarter than they think!
- They? What do you mean? Who?
- Ha-ha, I mean other people, the rest of the world, starting with your parents!
- You're an asshole.
- What do you think is the second margin to cut?
- The margin between you and a great mind?
- Almost!
- I knew it!
- That's the margin of the business itself!
- What do you mean?
- I mean reducing the fat, to go faster and then reach your goal faster.

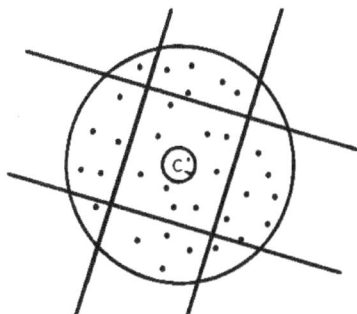

- So by reducing the second margin, the one inside the business, it reduces the margin outside the business, the one between where I am and where I want to go?
- Man, you're a genius! I should call Mr. Nobel to tell him to give you a prize!
- But how does it translate into reality?
- Concretely, I see 10 ways:

    1. Keep the people who adhere to the

company's core values and whose motivation is nourished.

2. Keep the activities that generate the most revenue, or the 20% that generate 80% of revenues.
3. Eliminate unnecessary activities, that is to say, all the ones that don't create profit today or tomorrow.
4. Outsource activities that cannot be eliminated but do not provide any real added value.
5. Increase investments. Keep good expenses. Eliminate bad ones.
6. Keep the best revenue streams as not all are equal. Predictable and recurring revenues are in every way superior to sporadic and contractual revenues.
7. For each product or service you offer, create a sub-company or a new brand to further specify its marketing positioning and characteristics; simplify the value proposition and be even more rooted in a small niche market.
8. Keep the most profitable and least demanding customers (in short, the best customers). You help them sleep better at night, right? So why should some customers keep you up at night?
9. Keep family and friends who encourage you. Leave aside those that pull you to the bottom. It's hard for them to see you change and succeed. Keep the spouse who will love you for who you are, and will support you during the highs as well as the lows. If she slows you down, reduce the margin and cut

her off.
10. Keep what works—stop refining and accelerate!

- Cut my girlfriend off, really?
- Is she a Piano Woman?
- She might have a big bucket, but not that much!
- Let me ask it differently: does she slow you down in your mission?
- I don't know, maybe a bit. I mean, she needs attention, we need to spend time together...
- Do you think she's the woman of your life?
- I don't know, I mean I'm only 21...
- That's what I said. So, in this process to reduce the margin, some core things will be kept, some useless things will be completely eliminated and some other things between will be recycled in Ctrl-N to create something new.
- Something new? You mean like a new product?
- That or a new added value to an existing one to satisfy more or get more customers. The most important thing to remember about reducing the margins of your company is that, in doing so, getting rid of distractions, you can focus more on your three keys to success:

1. Your business core: core people, core activities, core revenues, core expenses, core customers, core value proposition.
2. Your competitive advantage: the more you focus on your business core, the more you maximize it.
3. Your profit margin: the more you focus on your core and exploit your competitive advantage, the more you make money on

every product sold.

- Got it.
- And by doing so, I mean by reducing the margin within your company, you will get more speed.
- That's logical; it's like throwing the weight off a ship.
- Exactly! And more speed means a reduction in the outer margin: your road, and all that is on it, will shrink like in a funnel. Your peripheral vision will blur, and you'll have to put all of your energy into your business's vital functions. This is the same principle as the automation of the body in a position of danger. All of your efforts will serve to stay focused and keep the eyes right in front, on the goal. Once you feel it, mentally and physically, you know that your time is coming.
- My time? What do you mean?
- The time we call *The Nirvana of Business*.

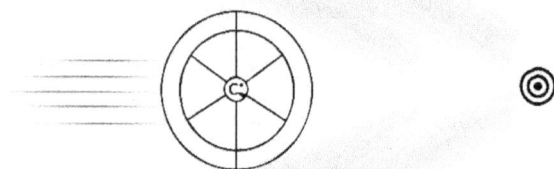

My turn

There are bad and good margins. 10% is a bad margin. 70% is a great margin. Now, who would settle for only a 10% margin?

Well, everyone who sells books through a publisher.

Publishers can take you into every store and make you sell a lot more books. But, most of the time, this is only true if you are famous, because most of the publishing companies won't invest a lot of money to market a "nobody". And most of them are bad at marketing, anyway.

From day 1, I didn't feel that I could justify letting a publishing company take roughly all my margin and my soul. As a humble and realistic guy, I don't think I will mass sell hundreds of thousands of copies anyway. So if I sell 5 000 copies—which is considered a best-selling book in Quebec, by the way—I prefer to get 70% of each sale. Wouldn't you?

Most of the entrepreneurs struggle to price their products. I think the margin approach is the best. Starting from my cost per unit, which is $5–$7, I've set my margins at 50–70%, but never below 50%, no matter the special sales I do. So that set the retail price around $25 CAD. The beauty of it is that with a 70% margin, my price is still competitive. Just a few products can aspire to the same *luxury*.

In the previous pages, we saw the internal and external margins. The obvious external margin that separates me from launching my book—after writing it, of course—was to get a publisher. I've cut this margin like the roughest haircut you never had.

An internal margin can't be relevant in the case of a book. But let me just say I've trashed almost half of everything I wrote for this book in order to stick to small chapters, leave room for illustrations and, overall, create an amazing user experience.

I heard a number of times that the difference between a good and a great book is often length: the shorter the better. You better finish reading the book with an "I want more" taste than an "I need to puke on Satan" feeling.

Your turn

The next chapter is a pause. It might sound weird to take a pause while you are going at lightning speed, but sooner or later, you will slow down. To support long-term growth, you need innovation.

That's why instead of getting rid of all of the good ideas and embryonic projects cut in the Ctrl-M – Reduce margins process, you need to keep them somewhere, on a blank page to be created here, on Ctrl-N – New. While Ctrl-M focuses on the short-term profitability, Ctrl-N focuses on the long-term growth.

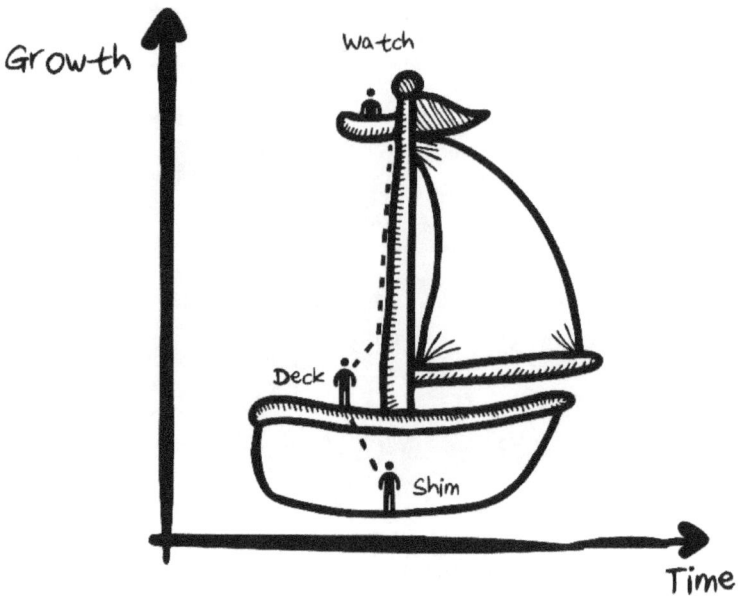

Ctrl-N: New

Reducing margins is a difficult exercise, and sometimes it can be heartbreaking—especially when it comes to throwing a promising project overboard: a new idea, activity, innovative process or any novelty really promising but slow to generate revenue or that is not consistent with your current core business.

That's why you need to press Ctrl-N and create a New Page.

This new page will serve as an idea box where you can list everything that could grow your business, like a new branch or a new business model.

This is a simple technique to innovate consistently and achieve sustained growth each year: the Blank Page strategy.

It is similar to the popular Blue Ocean Strategy, which illustrates the immense potential to create a new demand, in a strategic area where direct competition does not exist, and to write the rules of the game, with new activities that generate a value that goes beyond the traditional market segmentation.

The Blank Page Strategy recommends accomplishing something new or different on a regular basis. This is every day or week for some, every month for others; it allows you to grasp a new opportunity, regardless of the nature of the opportunity:

- New idea
- New feedback
- New demand
- New product
- New value
- New activity
- New process
- New revenue
- New model
- New strategy
- ...

However, keep in mind that this Blank Page Strategy is a long-running matter and that, on a daily basis, your focus should be on execution and profitability because without profit, you won't survive in the long run.

Or as Keynes said, in the long run, we are all dead!

Business model and long-term growth

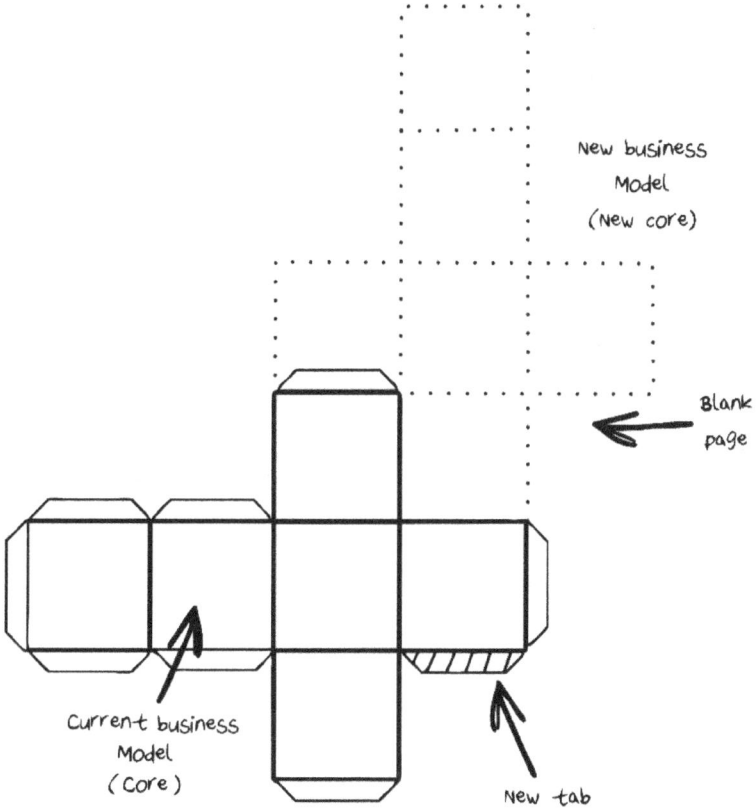

New business
Model
(New core)

Blank
page

Current business
Model
(Core)

New tab

Without innovation, you cannot reach the growth gap and go to the next level.

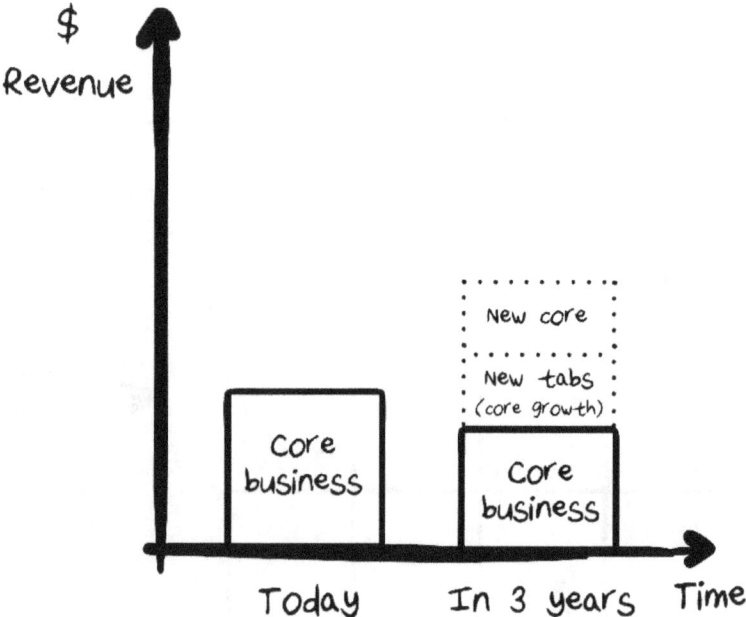

My turn

When you go high speed, get traction and attract more people to your thing, it's easy to lose focus and crash in a black hole.

The black hole here is the illustration of any other project you would like to start because you think you just had the idea of the century or because a bloodsucker magician made you buy what looked like a fantastic offer, at first.

This is why the exercise of the Ctrl-N shortcut is essential.

I live daily with some inside demons that always want to start things and never finish them. I bet we share the same demons.

That's why I try to list my new ideas on a blank page.

That allows me to flush them out of my head and sleep well knowing that they are safe on a new page. By the way, if you're scared of forgetting an idea, it means this idea probably sucks. When you're struck with a really good idea, you never forget it.

Their turn — CRTL-M-N

Here are the top 15 answers I got in my survey to the question: "How do you maximize profits?"

1. I decided to make my company invest in real estate to accumulate tangible and durable assets.

2. Buy things you really need and buy things you can put in your company's expenses. Other than that, invest money when you can.

3. People. Products. Profits.

4. Buy low, sell high (for example, buy oat, cotton or natural gas when it's low and sell higher).

5. Work in different places, reading about success and money, develop my network, go to special events and conferences, stay longer at work to meet people, give some of my time to talk about the projects and call clients.

6. Maximizing profits means questioning every expense in terms of ROI. If I need to spend a few hundred dollars on something that will make me gain double or triple the price, I call it an investment.

7. After designing over 1 000 websites, we not only learn about new technologies, but we also create new technologies and control them, so our costs are lower.

8. I charge more than a regular accountant as I have a specialization. I propose "packages" instead of hourly rates. Easier to have a bigger quote at the end.

9. We all work from home because Slack allows us to feel as if we are in the same room. We built an entire platform with pre-built tools without spending any money on coding.

10. Keep learning through experimentation. Bet big when you know it.

11. Weekly sales meetings with each venture, biweekly meetings with each venture for strategic decisions.

12. More effort on social media to get leads.

13. Keep cost down, invest in software and user experience.

14. More customers (fixed expenses).

15. We do not pay our employees less. But we do look for cheap rent either by inviting people to work remotely or even sharing space with other video game studios. We take advantage of regional tax credits in Canada. Leveraging these benefits is a huge advantage for our studio on the world stage and ensures we can hire top talent.

Your turn

MARKETING LAUNCH

So you've perfected the execution and focused on profits without forgetting long-term growth.

But who knows about it? Did you spread the news about your new business? Who will be there at your grand opening? What's your marketing strategy? Any guerilla plan?

a) I don't have any ideas yet.
b) Marketing is a word that means nothing. It's just a waste of time. And money.
c) I'll post it on Facebook and we'll see what happens.
d) Planning a launch is like planning the unpredictable; it confuses more than it helps.
e) My plan is to open my doors and wait for people to come in.
f) I'll pay someone for that.
g) None of the above.
h) All of the above.

H, really? You think because you've built a product and a company that your job is done? Too bad—the work has only just begun!

Ctrl-O: Open

Some people think marketing equals advertising. They maybe still live in the *good* old days when a few companies had all the money and power and controlled all forms of media.

Things have changed. Today, you don't need to spend a lot of money in advertising to launch something with a powerful marketing strategy. You just need two things: a damn great product that markets itself almost alone, and to OPEN.

You need to OPEN five things:

1. Open your doors—and release the Kraken!

It's time for the official marketing launch. Open the doors of your business, even if you don't have a storefront! The MVP has been refined, you have refocused around your core business, and you now have a company—not just a product. So, what are you waiting for? You can't be readier to open up to the world! Open your storefront, open your e-commerce shop, open your social media accounts, open everything that allows you to get in touch with people.

The "doors" here are only a metaphor, kind of. The mindset, though, is important. You know what you offer can make a positive difference in people's lives. Do not stay behind closed doors or deep in your basement. That would be selfish!

2. Open your heart.

It may sound melodramatic, but no matter the quality, the price, the Style or the prestige of your product, if you and every other person in your business, whether in contact with customers or not, don't keep an open heart, you won't keep your doors open for long.

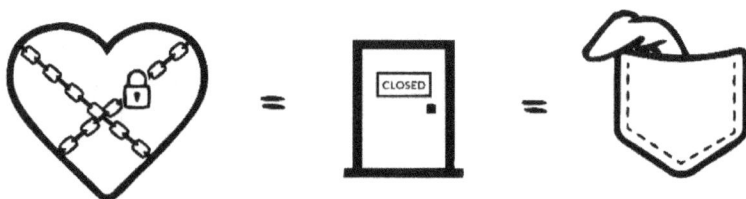

People buy with their hearts. They buy the person and his story, his service and generosity; in brief, they buy the human factor. Open your heart, and the gesture will be reciprocated. It is at this time when customers open their hearts that they become the ambassadors of your brand—they become the best customers, loyal, and, above all, the best salespeople!

3. Open your eyes.

Your doors and your heart are both open. Now look at what's happening around you. Pay attention to every move, every detail, as well as interactions between people in your business and your customers. Each of them. It's them who will tell you what to do next, and who will open your eyes to other opportunities. Don't close your eyes to what is bothering you, including things like the bad behaviour of an employee or a small defect in the product. Keep your eyes peeled!

4. Open your ears.

If you see what people are doing around you, but you don't listen to what they have to say, you're an idiot. You're losing all this valuable feedback for which large multinationals pay millions of dollars; it's called "rare commodity." The feedback is the heart of continuous improvement. Good feedback is gratifying and encouraging. Bad feedback should be even more welcome because it represents an opportunity to get better.

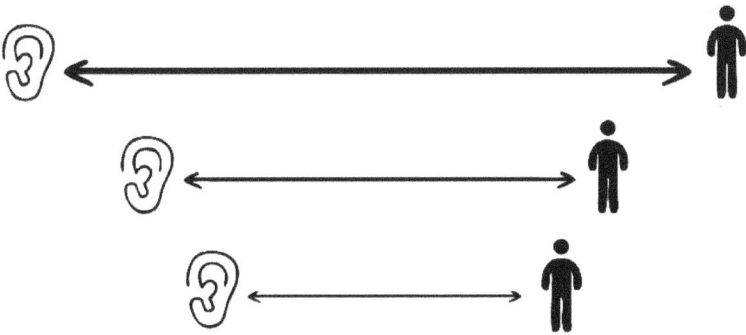

The shorter a feedback wave, the longer you stay close to the customer, the more you will succeed by adapting more quickly to their needs than large companies do. When they grow, companies generally lose this proximity with customers; the wave length of their feedback stretches. This leaves room for smaller players like you!

5. Open your mind.

You are engaged in an adventure where there is no path marked in advance. Stay alert and vigilant to any unforeseen circumstances or emergencies. But above all, stay open-minded to seize all the opportunities that will be more and more numerous as you progress. Experienced people say that opportunities arise in the action, but they arise firstly when your mind is open, at least enough to believe it. They also say that tomorrow anything can happen, and that's the beauty of it!

If you apply daily the five golden rules above, customers will come, and profits will follow.

P.S. Be sure to open one more thing:

6. Open a bank account, because dollars will rain, and you need to be ready to reinvest Ctrl-P.

My turn

I've reached this point. I was a few days away from officially launching my book. I considered different ways to launch it in an original way. Like to give 50% back to the first 100 buyers that write a review on Amazon—good or bad—and to auction off a few exclusive copies on Wallsh.com, a viral sale platform my team and I are building.

We'll see.

But for now, let's recap what I said in the Ctrl-O shortcut and apply it to my book:

Open my doors

- I sell books online. How can I open my doors?
- It's a metaphor, dude!

My doors are my website, my Amazon page especially, and every other place I can feature my book and sell it. And it's not because I sell online that I can't take orders offline! Every event I attend is like a storefront for me.

Open my heart

I tried to do it with this book, sharing my own and others' stories at the end of every chapter. And I reserved a little surprise for the launch.

Open my eyes

I've just seen defects in my book, a few English mistakes and an error in an illustration. I'll ask the proofreader and the designer to fix it.

Open my mind

I know it can't be perfect, but I'm a freak! I know I have to stop focusing on bugs if I don't want to become blind to everything else and miss the opportunities that arise.

Open my ears

What do you think about this book? I'm really curious, please tell me! Drop me an email at derekmorin.job@gmail.com

Open my bank account

It's open. But still empty. Come on money, don't be shy!

Your turn

Ctrl-P: Print

Imagine that your business is an amusement park, and you're about to open your doors. What is the first thing you would do?

- Make sure I have the newest and most beautiful rides?

You only need one super-fun ride.

- Make sure the ride is super safe?

You have created with all your heart something simple: an improved copy of another super-safe ride. Actually, if your product is endangering people's lives, then of course security is a must. But this is surely not the case. Your product is excellent. Stop being afraid.

- Ensure that there is enough food?

If you only have one ride, people won't eat there! And even if you had more rides, the food is incidental. The attraction is the ride, not the latest weird candy flavour on the market! In all cases, you can sell food later when your super-fun ride has brought enough people to justify and pay for the construction of a restaurant. But then, would you build a restaurant or a second ride?

- Ensure that there are kiosks to win doggies?

People play at kiosks only when the rides are boring. Yours is super fun. Stop focusing on extras. Remember

Ctrl-M and remain focused on your core: your simple and extraordinary ride.

- Ensure that people will not get lost on the site?

You only have one ride; how can people get lost?

- Make sure I have the best employees?

You only need one college dropout guy to watch the tycoon. Even though you'd have a lot of tycoons if the process is well-established and fine-tuned, do you really need a rare pearl at every position of your company to watch a tycoon? Just pick someone with a nice smile.

- Make sure I have the best prices?

Your tycoon is awesome. Customers will be ready to pay a lot to enjoy what you provide.

- Blah, blah, blah... fears, fears, fears... excuses, excuses, excuses...

Stop talking. Start selling!

SELL TICKETS!

This is the first thing you should do. The math is simple.

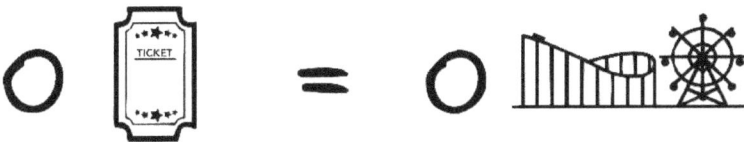

Actually, the calculation is the same for all companies, regardless of the type of business.

That is why the first thing to do is to press Ctrl-P and print tickets!

There are five things you need to Ctrl-P if you want your opening in Ctrl-O to be successful:

1. Print your product

Your business is probably not an amusement park, but let's say it is. Keep the focus on ticket sales of a super-fun ride that improves people's lives—even if it's only for 10 seconds. This message is not directed to crack dealers who already understand this principle.

2. Print your emotional footprint

Whether you're the owner of an amusement park or the employee who handles the ride, an insurance broker, a pharmaceutical representative or a shoe salesperson, people will always buy you before buying the product you sell. They will buy your personality, generosity, patience, service, your originality. They buy your personal trademark. So stop hiding behind your product. Show yourself up front and print your personal brand on people's hearts. Next time and every time thereafter they will need insurance, or shoes—no matter what you sell—they will first think of you, not of your product.

3. Print your story

To print your emotional footprint is more relevant for one-on-one meetings. In networking events, for example, people will buy a ticket for you because they had a good time by your side and kept good memories of you. Printing your story goes beyond one-on-one meetings; it extends to virally reaching people you do not know over the Internet and word of mouth—people who will comment and share your story with others. To print tickets for your story first means that you have a story. An ephemeral company has an ephemeral story. A great company has a great story. And a fantastic company—like Tom's, Zappos and Apple, to name a few—has a fantastic story.

- Yes, but I'm not Apple or any large successful company!
- You don't need to. You have your own fantastic story and you have built the foundation of your company on it: your personality, your interests, your competencies, your passion, your core and your bold purpose.

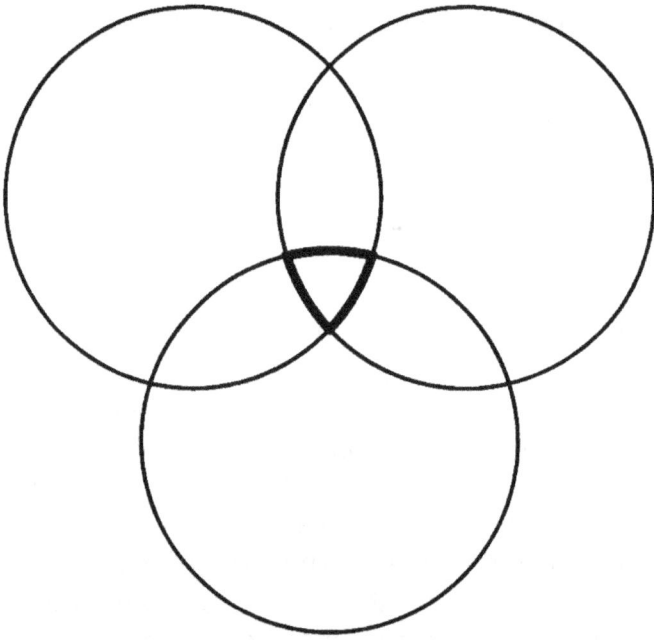

4. Print your passion.

"Print that shit out", as the Americans say. Spread it. A real passion is viral, by definition.

People think they have to invest a lot of money to market their product. That's one *lazy* way of doing things. But it's not the only way. For sure, printing beautiful and catchy ads and pasting them on the walls of buildings downtown can give your product the look of a rock star and help you sell a few more tickets. At least I hope so, with all the money you'll have to invest in the process!

The alternative is to follow the global trend of mass customization and self-publish your story with new

Internet platforms and new media, which are easily and freely accessible. This way there is no refusal, no waiting, no loss of motivation—you can print your own story for free or at a very low cost and promote it thanks to social networks or any other innovative way that did not exist the day before. Anyone can do it: your friends, your colleagues, your family—they can publish, print, promote for free on the Internet, but also in the streets and on the buildings' walls downtown!

- Yes, but printing is like killing a tree!
- So what? Printing can save a life, starting with yours!

5. Print things that work.

This step is easy. Print things that have given you success again and again. You did this, and it worked? Print it. That worked? Awesome! Print it.

My turn

Last time I went to an amusement park, I puked and almost ended up at the hospital after three tycoons. It was awesome!

They printed their emotional footprint so hard over my stomach, I felt bad for two days. But guess what I did when I recovered? Yeah right, I paid too much again to take a couple of tycoon rides and go back home sick right after.

I don't say you have to make people sick to reach success; I'm just a small bit of nature doomed to disappear, according to Darwin.

What I say is to bring so much emotion to your product that some people like me could fall for it and get sick, like sick of love.

If your product is shit, you won't get people sick in a good or a bad way. They will just ignore your products. And what's worst then being ignored? Nothing.

Actually, I'm wrong. Your product could be real shit and be awesome. A few months ago, I found a service called *Shit Express*. As the name suggests, it's a simple way to send a piece of shit in a box around the world. Within a few days, their shit-in-a-box delivery service went viral. Some crazy people like me loved it. Some other people were shocked— especially those who received a gift by mail. But overall, Shit Express is thriving because it's simple, innovative, and it responds to a need. Opinions differ on which need, however!

I see this Ctrl-P shortcut as a checklist.

✓ Print my product?

I was a few days away from finally printing my book.
Actually, it's print-on-demand: you buy it, they print it and
ship it. Part of my product is also the web page I built to
promote it and the coupon code I shared with the first
buyers. I've also *printed* a promotion to lather up the
marketing at launch: the first 100 buyers who write a decent
review, good or bad, will get 50% of their money back. It's a
win-win because they will get the book for free (they will
only pay shipping cost), and I will sell a lot more copies
because of their reviews.

✓ Print my emotional footprint?

I'm not the most charismatic guy on earth. But I do believe
people listen when I talk, even if two-thirds of what I say is
pure but funny bullshit. Maybe it's because what I say is
different. Maybe it's because they are tired of talking about
the weather. Or maybe it's because people like to be
entertained. Yeah, got it. I think that's the main reason you
bought this book. Will you buy the next one?

✓ Print my story?

This is literally what I did. The expression remains to be
taken figuratively, though! What's the story behind your
product? Why did you build it? Far beyond a cheap price and a
good service, this is the main reason people will pay for it.

✓ Print my passion?

Spending all my evenings and weekends for months to write this book was exactly that, a print of my passion. Without passion, I would have probably given up. At best I would have chosen 100 times out of 100 to spend my sunny Sundays on a boat and not in a basement with no window. Maybe you won't like the fruit of my passion like I hate passion fruit, but you won't deny you feel the sweat I put into this book.

✓ Print things that work?

Things that work could be huge and tiny things. A huge thing for me was to make the whole analogy of the keyboard shortcuts to work almost flawlessly with business.

A tiny thing in appearance but huge in the end was the following one. Like every author, I've been stuck a lot of times with the blank page problem. One day I wrote non-stop for six hours without any pause. And not just crappy content, there was good stuff too. The day after, the same thing! And then I realized that every time I was listening to the Above & Beyond *Group Therapy* album, I was super-focused and productive.

Their turn — Ctrl-O-P

Here are the top 12 answers I got in my survey to the question: "When you officially launched your business, what key marketing efforts paid off the most?"

1. One of the things I do with my business is creating business speed dating events. I am printing real tickets and my story as well. After the events, participants bring the story of my business home, and it is impacting their buying mindset.

2. Telling all my contacts that I'm available for work. If you did a good job for them, they will find jobs for you. What you did in the past is what is going to sell you in the future. Let everybody know what you can do and how you can help them.

3. Business stickers, and just putting myself out there. Design, luckily, is a "sexy" career to have, and more often than not people are curious about what I do.

4. Ha! All I can say is try a few methods cheaply. Pay attention to conversions and double down where things are looking good and keep optimizing. With that being said, competitive advantages are not made in doing many channels and optimizations at once. Advantages are built by truly understanding your customers and your product positioning. If you really get those two things, the channels that should give you the most leverage will become obvious.

5. What helped the most was starting an online presence and writing about my expertise. My worst marketing effort was newspaper advertisement: no ROI because my services were not designed for the general public. Specialized magazines probably would have been better, but their costs were way too much for my budget at the time.

6. Business networking always works for us. Get out and meet people who will not only be your clients but also be your business allies. Also, constantly performing online marketing through Facebook, Twitter, YouTube videos and other social media is important. We send out a newsletter both online and paper. We keep our blogs up to date to stay on top of Google searches. We appear as public speakers because that puts us in front of our potential clients and proves our value proposition to our market.

7. I made a big opening with the mayor, my clients, my business partners and friends. That was big and very helpful. Social networks and our website were the best.

8. Email advertising and the later use of social networks worked effectively for me. But, for a long time, one of my mistakes was that I was offering training courses for highly skilled people instead of offering adapted training for beginners. My competitors were offering numerous training courses for beginners, and once they were hooked, they continued to make the other levels of training (which are more profitable). So now I am addressing this old problem by targeting the beginners first! And it works!

9. Validation and feedback from sending out surveys through our marketing channels.

10. Getting the right co-founders.

11. I was asked to be a key speaker at a local festival of video games and animation just after our first studio was getting up and running. I decided to speak about our approach to corporate culture and team-building for creative engineering teams. As a result of that talk, I was inundated with resumes from would-be game programmers and artists who said things like "Finally! A studio that gets it!"

12. Using ASO (app store optimization), social media ads for downloads, email marketing, and some form of print advertising when the budget allows.

Now you: what are the huge and tiny things that work just great for you?

Your turn

FINE-TUNING

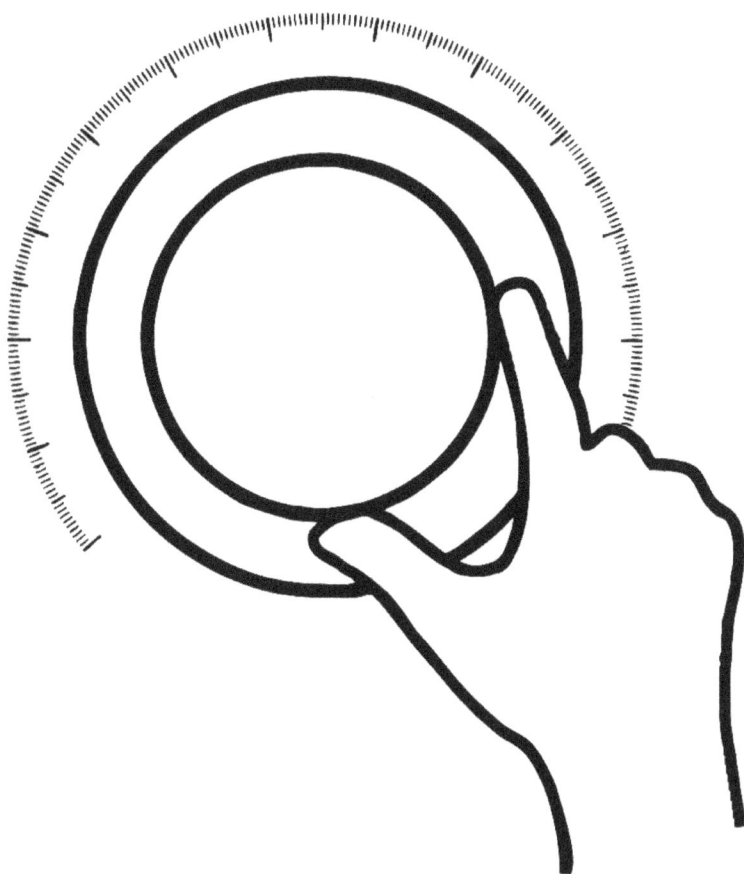

So you've done a powerful marketing launch and you're looking for the next move to do. But what should it be?

a) I'll wait for results.
b) Why more? Why not less?
c) I'm too busy fulfilling the current demand.
d) Everything is perfect. I won't touch anything.
e) I'll start another business.
f) I'll retire. I'm rich enough.
g) None of the above.
h) All of the above.

Please answer G and turn the page.

Ctrl-Q: Quit

- Why quit? This is only the beginning!
- Wait, I'll tell you...

Quit.

For most people, this word is a synonym of failure.

quit   fail

If you think like these people, please unsubscribe to this belief!

Here's the funny story of a friend of mine, who once changed his belief:

The last time I went to see a movie, I left the room after just 30 minutes. Yes, I admit, I quit... The film was stinky, and I had 1 000 more important things to do! Actually, sleep would have been a better thing to do than watching this crappy movie, but with all the noise in the room, I could not sleep, so I had to quit. Am I a loser for so little? During this time I saved, I could work on my business, schedule an appointment, find a new customer, sell... but instead of that, I made a list of everything I had to quit. Here it is:

30 things I have to quit to succeed and be happy before my 30th birthday

☐ 1. Procrastination, cowardice, lack of effort and all that leads to it—any activity or any excuse. How can you dream of success and sleep well when you know that by working smarter, every day, you can be successful? If you do not start today, you never will end tomorrow. Sometimes it's good to dream, but more often it's better to wake up. Not convinced? Check out Shia Lebeouf's speech on YouTube. Do it.

☐ 2. The inability to make decisions is connected to procrastination. What is common to all people who are successful is making decisions quickly and changing their minds—the few times they do this—rarely and slowly. The opposite is true for people who are not successful: they make decisions slowly and change their minds quickly and often.

☐ 3. Impatience, intolerance, intemperance, incoherence, inconsistence and all other flaws that sound like "ence." Even flatulence.

☐ 4. TV. Find one person who is successful that watches TV three hours per day. Good luck.

☐ 5. Past. To focus on the big picture of the future; to work on one thing at a time and finish it!

☐ 6. Elsewhere. Live your life here, today. Do not escape

to an exotic region; do not dream of your next holiday, because you are at work! And if you don't have any upcoming holidays, that's great news! It means you work hard, and success is knocking at your door.

☐ 7. The status quo. Do not be afraid of or fight against change, because it is inevitable! It's like fighting against yellow. It's a lost cause—I mean, that's a primary color! For sure you'll finish second! The only way to grow is by seeing and doing things differently. The good, as well as the bad, always ends up changing; it's inevitable, as sunrise breaks the status quo of the night.

☐ 8. The old patterns that keep you in the status quo and mediocrity. Stop thinking that the things you have always done in the same way must be done again and again the same way. There are always other options. You can't expect new results with old patterns. Isn't that the definition of insanity by Albert Einstein? Experiment. Take risks. It will make you feel alive.

☐ 9. The victim feeling. We are all victims of the sexual act of our parents. Thus, we are born. For everything else, you can't use the victim role to procrastinate. Playing the victim often has a cousin: putting the blame on others. Others do not care about you anyway. They do not care what you have, what you don't have, or how you feel. By blaming others, you deny your responsibility for what happens to you and so you perpetuate the problem. Blaming is an excuse and the best recipe for failing miserably. Always repeat that to yourself; you will pay more attention to your destiny, of which you are the master.

☐ 10. Negativity. People are not attracted to negativity. Success comes through the cooperation of people when they surround us. And only positive people attract people.

☐ 11. Bad habits. To succeed, you must be healthy. Quit addictions such as alcohol, gambling, cigarettes, etc.

☐ 12. The ego and vanity. Some people believe that power and ego are related. What about Nelson Mandela, Gandhi, or Mother Teresa?

☐ 13. The desire to impress others. Do it for you. Others don't care about you, anyway.

☐ 14. Jealousy or trying to be someone else. It sounds simple, but it is probably the most difficult thing: be yourself in a world that is trying to make us all the same. It is easy to change to be loved by others. But why? Someone will always be more beautiful, smarter, happier, younger than you. Why not be yourself then!? This is the only way that good and like-minded people are going to like you, not those people you want love from, who in reality are not like you at all! Do you like this book? Do not be jealous! Be inspired and create an improved copy of it. Are you envious of him or her? Same principle.

☐ 15. The frustration. People will make you angry, so just don't answer them or reply with a smile. I have been told that we can differentiate a good entrepreneur from a great entrepreneur because we made him eat shit, and he asks for more with a smile.

☐ 16. The desire to control everything. This is the cousin of being over-cautious, which leads to the inability to take risks, which leads to being conservative and watching your competitors thrive while you sit in the status quo. Let's add in that some things deserve your control, but some don't. If you want to control everything, you get into a life of eternal anxiety and an inability to trust anyone. This leads to another scourge: the inability to cooperate and delegate. Keep in mind that you cannot control external circumstances, but you can control your reaction. Invest your energy into what you can control. Your business, for example... not the NASDAQ!

□ 17. The losers around you. If you hang out with nine losers, you will be the 10th, for sure.

□ 18. Always say yes. This is the best way to fail to do what you promise. And it's the best way to anger and disappoint others. One yes for nine no's—this is the key to success. Referring to #17 above, every yes in contrast to your alignment pulls you away from your mission. Life is limited. Never forget that.

□ 19. Gossip. Speaking about nothing and worrying about nothing. Leave these activities to immature young girls on reality shows.

□ 20. Too much care to "juice-sucking" customers that siphon 80% of your energy for only 20% of your profits.

□ 21. Fill all of your free time. You know the story of the guy who thinks he is super busy and seems to be to those who see him, but who merely fills all his free time with unnecessary actions because he is too lazy to leave his comfort zone and do something that will ultimately have an impact on his life and other people's lives? Follow what the client needs first, not what you impose on yourself as a workload without a valid reason, nor the profit at the end of the line.

☐ 22. Buy unnecessary things. Happiness is not in the property. It is in the action. Spend your money on things important to you: a trip, organic food, an opportunity. Actually, don't spend—invest in things you keep. See all expenditures as an investment, and if it bothers you, it's because this is probably not an investment.

☐ 23. Any distraction that goes against your goal. Focus on one thing and one thing only, and do it well. This includes your boyfriend/girlfriend. If he/she slows you down instead of propelling you forward, or if his/her fundamental view of life is different from yours, then say like James Blunt: "Goodbye, my lover."

☐ 24. Fears and superstitions (those are the sum of ignorance and fear). We have six visceral fears, which are poverty, criticism, ill health, the loss of love, old age and death. It is normal to be afraid, to be anxious, scared, to have secrets, we're human! What is bad is when fear gets out of hand and takes control of your mind and your body. The main and most fatal fear for the entrepreneur: the fear of failure. Why be afraid to fail? You are the underdog versus failure, which will win four times out of five against you, if not more! So if you rely on statistics, you will fail. Knowing this, how can you be afraid? What makes people scared is the unknown, but here you know the end of the story, 80% of the time! What if that was the beauty of launching something? Being the underdog and having everything to gain. Knowing that you have four chances out of five to fail, imagine how great the remaining chance tastes when it materializes into success!

☐ 25. The part-time job that makes you feel secure. Job stability = poor life. Zero risk = zero success. Quit salary for income. Be committed 100% to the project, not 100% to being a grocery clerk!

☐ 26. The lack of ambition. This means to profoundly change your beliefs and replace your "I was born to lose" inner voice with an "I was born to succeed" one. It also may mean changing groups of friends, leaving your city, state, province or country.

☐ 27. Phrases like "I can't, I must not, I should not" and all words ending with *not* or *'t* or anything that sounds like excuses. "I can't do it, I'm unable!" You're probably right; eight out of ten times you will fail, but remember that the best baseball players earn trophies by succeeding only three out of ten times trying to hit the ball! To fail is an almost compulsory road to success full of learning that only the act of falling can teach us. The real failure is not to try.

☐ 28. Bad partners, both personal and professional. Whether your business partner, co-founder, investor with whom you have an irreparable dispute or your family members that take you down unconsciously because they do not like seeing you change or want to protect you from failure, unhappiness destroys ambition.

☐ 29. Don't be ordinary. Be different. Be weird. Don't just be *good enough*—be extraordinary. People treat you how you want to be treated. They will treat you *good enough* if you believe you are. Don't wait for the approval of a superior officer or a parent or anyone to do an action. Apologize if you make a mistake, but do not ask for permission. Take the initiative.

☐ 30. Quit what you are doing now—reading this damn chapter—and go outside. Build your business as it should be. Come on, do it!

Here is a simple way to quit what slows you down.
Complete the lines below.

WHO	WHY	WHAT	WHEN
Your name	*Health*	*Cigarette*	*Oct 12th, noon*
_____	_____	_____	_____
_____	_____	_____	_____

The date and time are super important. This is the
moment when you'll refresh your pattern to start on a
new basis. This exercise is not only good for yourself; it
is also crucial for your business.

WHO	WHY	WHAT	WHEN
(Employee name)	*Pain for the team*	*Company*	*Right away!*
Production team	*Lose money*	*Website design*	*15/01/2016*
_____	_____	_____	_____
_____	_____	_____	_____

If you quit all that slows you down and diverts you
from your path to success, things are now likely aligned
right!

My turn

During the last years, I worked out.

Of course you could say I wear a small belly, I have no muscle, don't look in shape at all and my face full of dark circles looks ill. You would be right!

I didn't work out in a gym—except to get the newspaper for free, once—and I do too little sport.

I worked out to quit as many things as possible from the 30 things to quit before 30.

To be honest, I still struggle with a lot of them, on a daily basis. I think that's human nature.

One thing for sure, everybody is sleeping on this promising Saturday. It's barely 7 AM, and I'm alone in a coffee shop finishing the last details of this book.

Now you: which of the 30 things to quit before 30 did you overcome? Which one is still your nightmare?

Your turn

Ctrl-R: Refresh and Align right

Ctrl-R involves two very important actions that allow you to restore order and move on to another level, a new level of growth: Refresh and Align right.

Refresh

You have:

- *Ctrl-O*: Officially opened the doors of your business.
- *Ctrl-P*: Printed and have sold tickets!
- *Ctrl-Q*: Quit what slowed you down so you could jump to another level.

The time has come to Ctrl-R: Refresh.

After each period of intense sprint, or after each Ctrl-Q, take a short break. Rest. Take a nap, take part in a refreshing activity, like climbing, kite surfing or walking. Take this exercise seriously. Depression or exhaustion can hit you sneakily, without warning. Schedule this refresh exercise often, at least once a week. Plan a time during the week, a time slot reserved only for that and nothing else.

In Ctrl-Q, you committed to leaving all these old patterns, and all these distractions that slow you down. Obviously, this will not happen overnight. The important thing is to give yourself a deadline and to respect it. Be honest with yourself, because this deadline will be the time you will Press Ctrl-R to refresh these patterns kept hidden in your system.

"But why and how do we do it?" You might ask.

To survive and grow, it is essential to refresh the four keys below to align right, both for yourself and your business:

1. Internal Program
2. Appearance
3. Energy
4. Purpose

Why refresh yourself?

Six reasons:

1. You feel exhausted and on the edge of depression.
2. Your face looks like a zombie.
3. Your body says, "Stop!"
4. You do not feel aligned with your goals.
5. You are wondering why you get up every morning.
6. You feel as if you are not going in the right direction or getting anywhere.

Don't try to do everything, because you won't be able to; you'll feel incompetent and lose confidence. So the vicious circle goes on! Instead, be sure to delegate.

Why refresh your business?

Five reasons:

1. A member of your team is not compatible with the others or is not in the right place in the company.
2. Your product needs a facelift, a new packaging, refinement.
3. You don't feel the *flow*; there's a lack of challenge or a feeling of incompetence.
4. Your business is not going in the right direction.
5. Your product, service, your approach, or whatever, is not up to date.

Press Ctrl-R.

- Refresh your browser and update your internal program, which indicates the way to follow and allows you to be functional on a daily basis.
- Refresh your energy: take a break, clear your thoughts, sleep.
- Refresh your appearance: increase your confidence and the confidence of others, increase sales—in short increase all that is positive.
- Refresh your goal.

Align right

The idea is to align the right personal and professional goals with your priorities, which are non-negotiable.

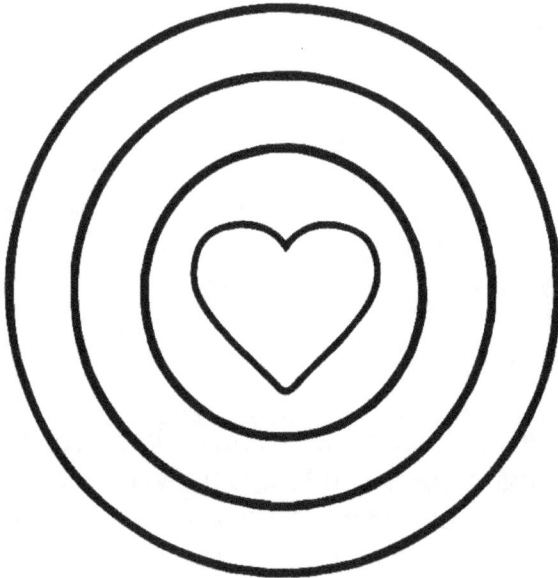

Aligning a business's goals with its priorities is to design a living on what is important and meaningful today; this is non-negotiable and will remain that way.

Here's a thought that summarizes the whole concept:

It's not about doing everything right;
it's about being aligned right,
going in the right direction,
doing the right thing.

Let's dissect this thought:

It's not about doing everything right: the worst of all scourges is to try to do everything perfectly. This results, most of the time, in doing nothing at all.

It's about being aligned right: it says what it has to say! However, here's another way to illustrate the importance of being aligned right. In the diagram at the end of this chapter, taken from the *Blue Ocean Strategy*, to be aligned right means to eliminate obsolete or useless things, to reduce what could be more advantageous to have a smaller amount, or to increase what would make you stand out from competition and create what would make you and your company a unique player.

One could argue that the ideal is for you to be right-aligned—that is to say, in the RAISE and CREATE boxes in the illustration at the end of this chapter, because this is where the added value is created and gives a reason for you and your company to exist.

Going in the right direction: What are your goals? Do you know the destination of where you are heading at full speed? Often people set too many goals, which are either too low or too high, which affects the motivation to achieve them. To stay focused, the simplest way is to align yourself with one single key metric. Want to grow your business by 100% this year? Perfect!

Assume the simplest key metric to determine whether or not you are achieving your goal: revenue. And put the emphasis solely on this metric. It may sound simplistic, but too many people let themselves be distracted by several other metrics that do not indicate if you are going in the right direction: the number of partners, the number of visits to your website, the number of minutes spent on each page, the number of calls, the number of customers, the number of this, the number of that... You'll lose your mind trying to track, analyze, and especially grow every number of every key metric. So put the emphasis on one, and if you do not know which one, you can't be wrong by choosing the revenue!

Of course, depending on where you are in your development phase and your business model, this key metric may change. For example, a digital startup can have as its only key metric the number of free subscriptions on its website, and then in the future try to monetize those users with a premium account or advertising. Or a mature company could have the expenses as the only key metric, to limit or reduce them and thus greatly increase profits for its shareholders. But this is probably not the case for you yet!

Doing the right thing: You will have good and bad shots. You will often proceed by trial and error to achieve your goal. You can't go against the law of statistics: the more you try, the more you will make mistakes.

However, the more you make mistakes, the more you learn, the better you become and the more you will do the right thing. For this logic to be respected, though, for every action you make, good or bad, you have to Ctrl-S: Save it.

Refresh things at left; align right for growth

Eliminate	Raise
Reduce	Create

My turn

Sorry guys, I took a break for this one.

Like I said in the Ctrl-R shortcut a bit earlier:

It's not about doing everything right: I can skip writing for once.

It's about being aligned right: Never been more laser-focused.

Going in the right direction: Right ahead, to help me thrive.

Doing the right thing: I feel like it's the right thing. Sales will prove me right, I guess.

Their turn — Ctrl-Q-R

Here are the top 15 answers I got in my survey to the question: "Name at least one thing you had to quit and/or to align right in to succeed (personal or business point of view)."

1. I'm not watching TV anymore. I always try to save time to focus on my business and to get proper sleep at night. I had some people around me who were accusing me of being a dreamer, that I will get screwed and blah-blah. You know what? I burned bridges with them! I quit the negative people! Then, I took the decision to organize my own networking activities for serious business people only, even if I needed to build my own private club!

2. Finding the right partners. It had taken many tries before I knew what I really wanted and what I really needed. When you define yourself, you can find partners who think and work like you. When you find them, it's like finding a gold mine.

3. My job! I was stuck in a place that didn't value quality and was bent solely on maximizing profits.

4. Your people. Everyone is moving so quickly that it's hard to keep them going as a group in one direction. Sometimes this means letting people go. Sometimes this means letting yourself go. If you've seen *Mighty Ducks*, you might remember a scene where everyone is tied together going in his own direction and falls down. The key is getting everyone to align at a high

level to travel together, even if the individual paths aren't exactly aligned.

5. Jobs that don't really fit with my goals, that don't give me many opportunities and where the salary is bad.

6. When I started, I made two mistakes: wrong clients (they just did not want to invest in improving their knowledge!) and jumping in a big contract with one big client that kept me busy almost all the time. When he pulled the plug, I was left with no projects and no prospects.

7. I never stop to have a life because I have a business. I have two kids (piano, gymnastics 16 hours per week), so I'm very busy. I'm training six days a week (1 hour of intense training). Plus I'm running. I NEVER stop anything. I have to think about myself. This is important. Training keeps me alive. I'm more efficient and can concentrate better.

8. Quit my ex-husband...(joking! But it helped a bit!). In fact, when I moved from my small house to the new big house, the perception of my clients changed and the business got better!

9. To understand that success is a result of failing in the right direction. And never giving up.

10. Quit drinking, so that I can learn more.

11. Social life.

12. Health or personal life. Choose.

13. Control.

14. Set big and vague goals (instead of stupid S.M.A.R.T. ones) and then only worry about the next step. And the next. And the next. If you don't know what the next step is, go have a coffee with someone you've been meaning to have a coffee with and see how you can help them. You'll come out of it with that next step. 2) Forget about who you are and what you can or can't do: it's not about you but about who you can help.

15. "The right people in the right seats". We had hired a talented, extremely experienced triple-A art director early in the company. As he began to apply slow, bureaucratic and 'large studio' practices to our small, elite team of agile developers, it became clear that there wouldn't be a fit. We attempted to help him adapt, but he insisted on doing it his way, which wasn't what the team wanted. We let him go, and the team felt unleashed. Productivity went up; quality improved and nobody missed the extra work he'd had them doing. I had to quit worrying about how and why I should do this and dedicate the time I needed to get it done. Which is still a work in progress.

Your turn

LONG-TERM GROWTH

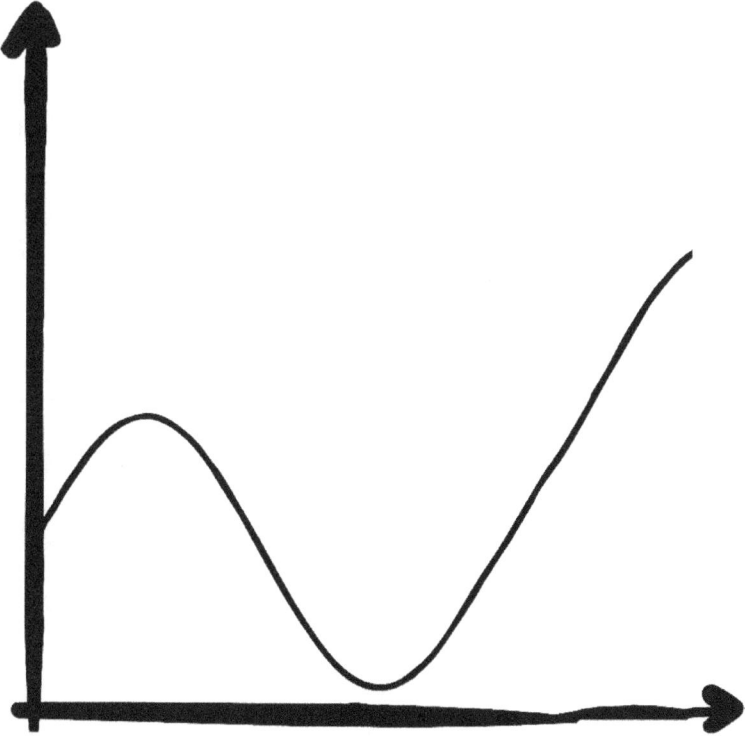

So you've perfected the execution, quit things that slowed you down and refreshed and re-aligned your priorities with your goals, and now you want to reach the next level of growth.

What will you do next?

a) Explore new ideas.
b) Try new processes.
c) Prototype new products.
d) Launch a new brand to target a younger market.
e) Dig for more capital.
f) Acquire another smaller business.
g) None of the above.
h) All of the above.

As you move forward, it seems like choices are smarter, business-wise. Just like you!

Ctrl-S: Save

Each time you make an action, regardless of the
outcome, no matter the magnitude, save it. In his
famous book *The Lean Startup*, Eric Ries explains the
importance of quickly accumulating feedback from
customers, doing so frequently, saving it and learning
from it to make important decisions brighter, more
frequent and faster. Basically, all decisions come down
to whether you need to:

1) Persevere in this direction

OR

2) Pivot in another direction

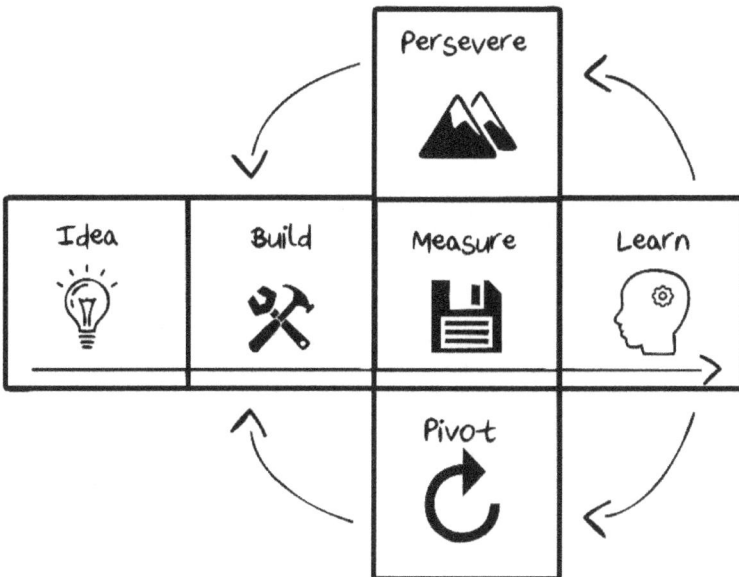

Save the data you need to learn and make a decision: to persevere or to pivot.

Again, there are so many different types of data you can save. But, as mentioned in Ctrl-R, build upon one single key metric at a time, the most important one in the development phase where you are now.

Otherwise, you'll go crazy with the hundreds of different data sources and get paralyzed when the time comes to make an important decision. It will save you time, money and energy—the three crucial elements you absolutely need to save.

If this key metric is not enough, look at the second key metric in importance. But do it only if truly necessary, to avoid stunning yourself with data that anyone can say anything about!

So, save what's important—really important—and get rid of the rest. Take the weight off. Stay lean in your business and your life to have the flexibility to pivot quickly and often. Staying lean can take many forms: small teams, little or no debt, little equipment.

Don't build an elephant.

Speaking of this, Gerd Gigerenzer sounds like an animal species, but he's actually an author. An awesome one, actually. In his book called *Gut Feelings: The Intelligence of the Unconscious*, which was Malcolm Gladwell's inspiration for his bestseller *Blink*, Gerd Gigerenzer uses a quick and simple decision tree to make decisions... complex and vital ones!

One of the most striking examples of his book is the decision tree to manage patients suffering from heart attacks to reduce the number of errors and death.

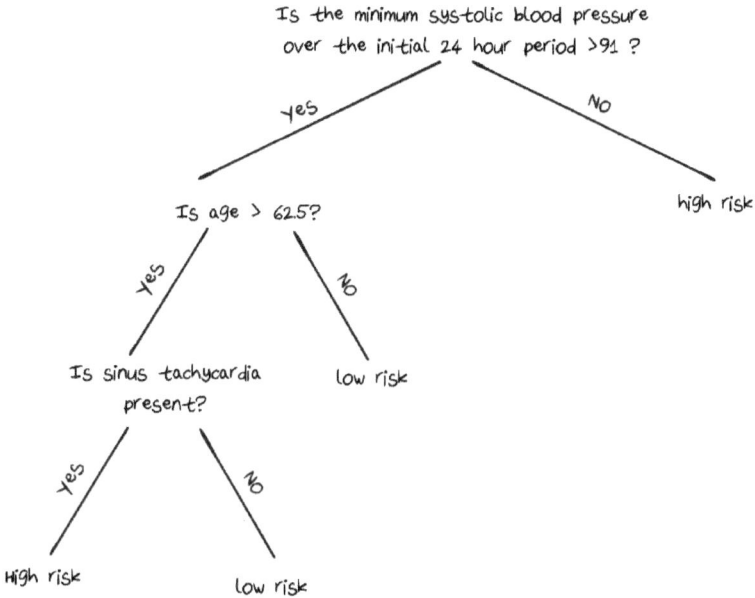

Is the minimum systolic blood pressure over the initial 24 hour period >91 ?

yes → Is age > 62.5?

No → high risk

Is age > 62.5?
yes → Is sinus tachycardia present?
No → low risk

Is sinus tachycardia present?
yes → High risk
No → low risk

Some people say, "Hey! That's too simple; it is unwise to play with people's lives like that!"

Well, they might ignore that this *simple and stupid* decision tree has saved hundreds of thousands of lives! And it's now the methodology to follow in almost every hospital on earth.

This is why I copied it to create an improved version for a business that every entrepreneur should assimilate. Here's the decision tree of business:

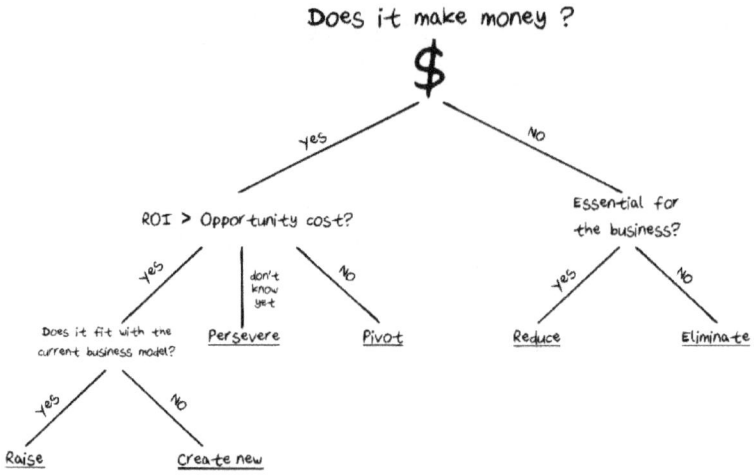

Does it make money?

$

yes / NO

ROI > Opportunity cost?

Essential for the business?

yes / don't know yet / NO

yes / NO

Does it fit with the current business model?

Persevere

Pivot

Reduce

Eliminate

yes / NO

Raise

Create new

My turn

To persevere or to pivot. To be or not to be. Same fight.

Throughout the writing process, I've accumulated a lot of files on my computer that I tried to organize by throwing them all in a folder. With so much data—mostly useless—it's so easy to lose focus on what's important: sales.

From day one, I knew my high concept was selling by itself. But to know it and to live it are two worlds. As long as nobody gives you cold hard cash for your product, you have nothing but a dream. And unless you're Walt Disney, chances are you can't eat if your dream remains a dream.

Here's the *Lean Startup* loop I made to quickly measure the potential of this book.

1. <u>Idea</u>: Keyboard shortcuts to success—people might think my idea was the book itself, but the book is only a means to communicate the real idea, like any other means: conference, video, app, webinar, workshop, etc.

2. <u>Build</u>: I built the framework based on my high concept and I wrote the first pages. From then, I spent more time on building the Kickstarter campaign and marketing it than I did working on the book itself. I don't say you should work less on your product and deliver shit with a fantastic marketing campaign. I'm just saying don't think that once you build the product your job is done, because it just begins! That being said, it's smart to spend less time building the product at first and more time to market

it, getting feedback, improving it, making some sales and justifying the need for your product.

3. <u>Measure</u>: My key metric was not the traffic on the Kickstarter page, nor the number of times my video was seen, nor the number of Likes or Comments or Cheers. My only metric was the number of sales.

4. <u>Learn</u>: I've learned a lot of things. But the one that excited me the most and the cornerstone of my decision to persevere and not to pivot was the number of sales from non-friends and non-family members: close to 75%.

5. <u>Persevere</u>: "Maybe my book could be really good, I told myself, and people buy it because they like it, not because it's me, and they pity me".

6. <u>Build</u>: I wrote this book.

From this point, I need your feedback and insights. Then I'll validate my next move based on the decision tree of business, seen earlier in Ctrl-S.

Your turn

Ctrl-T: New tab

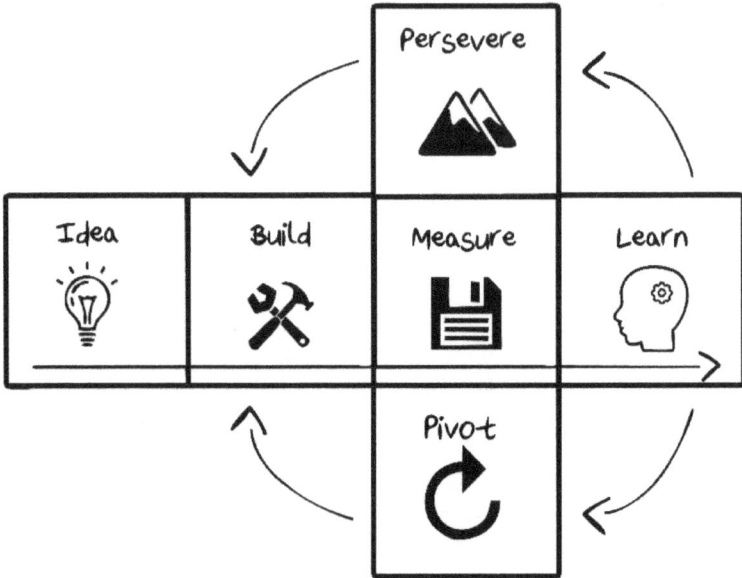

Every time you follow the building process above, you will need to open one or more new tabs to test different alternatives, eliminate most, validate some and integrate them within the business or keep them apart, for later or for another project/company.

- What's a tab?

In a web browser, you open a new tab to navigate to a new page without leaving the current one. This is the same principle in business.

You can open a new tab to explore new business opportunities without leaving the current window of opportunity, your core business that pays the bills each month.

Your core is stable and works almost automatically— that is to say that your business can operate without you and make money while you are away or sleeping. This is what differentiates businesses from crafts.

Since you are a visionary entrepreneur, you now enjoy more free time to open new tabs so you can explore new avenues for growth.

- Why open a new tab, and why now?

Do you want to drive a thriving business and innovate constantly to dominate your niche market? If the answer is yes, open new tabs, one to begin with.

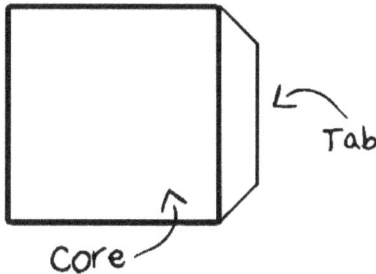

The tab is the side of the business model, within the company but on the sidelines. That's the difference between Ctrl-T: Open a new tab and Ctrl-N: Open a new page, which may mean a new business model, a new brand, a new branch—in short, a new entity. The tab is the side of a window that so perfectly illustrates the lateral thinking, at the basis of innovation.

Opening a new tab allows your company to keep an eye and observe carefully:

- The value proposition
- Customers
- Competition
- The market
- Employees
- Partners
- Novelty
- Opportunities

It is a way to innovate at the margin of the core, without putting the company at risk, both financially and in terms of reputation. This principle applies to all business spheres.

Here's how it works.

You want to try something new? A new process, new employee, new market, new package, new billing type...

You open a new tab to explore, test and validate if it works or not. It's like opening a small test cell to build a prototype and test it on a small amount of people with multiple iterations and adjustments, like explained by the Ctrl-F-G-H loop.

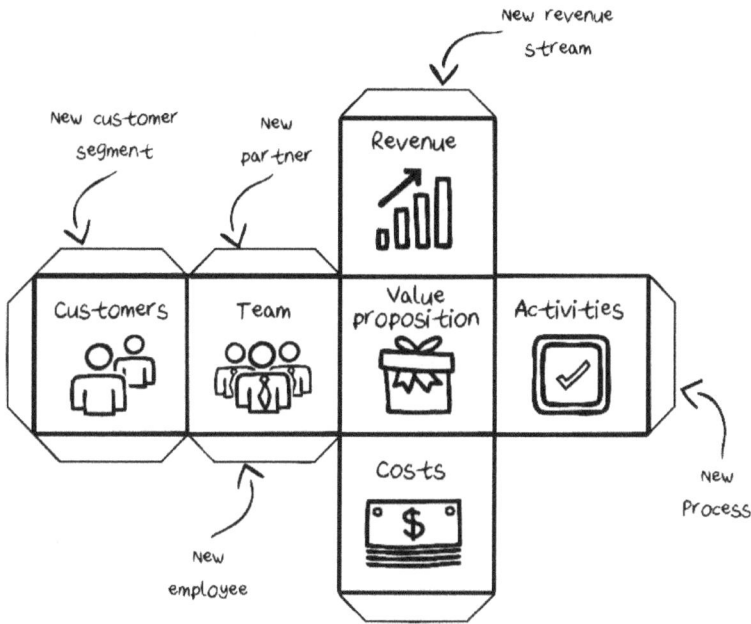

You can open multiple tabs at once, but it's risky. It requires more energy, more people and more money. If you are alone, it is a bad idea because you will eventually destroy yourself. It's not recommended either if you are just starting out as an entrepreneur; it will make you lose focus. But as you grow, new tabs are your business's main long-term source of growth.

To validate the relevance of this new tab, if it should stick or be cut, I created the decision tree of Innovation:

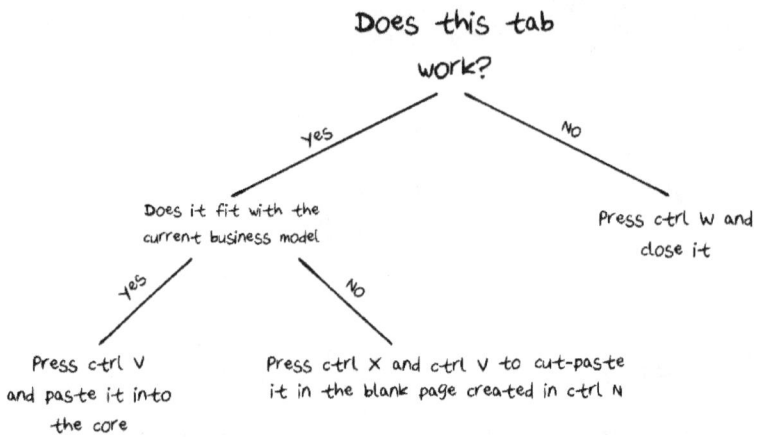

Does this tab work?

yes — Does it fit with the current business model

No — Press ctrl W and close it

yes — Press ctrl V and paste it into the core

No — Press ctrl X and ctrl V to cut-paste it in the blank page created in ctrl N

My turn

Since I'm still writing these lines, and I didn't publish the book yet, I can't know if the new tabs will work. And it's too early to implement new tabs before the market validates that my core business is solid.

Creating new tabs is an important process to stay open-minded and ready to seize opportunities. So the exercise for me is more like a theoretical one than a practical one. But trust me, I know that if I don't map all the opportunities in new tabs on a piece of paper, I might be blind to the massive source of revenues.

Here are a few new tabs I expect to test and validate in the following months.

Customers:

- Schools
- Companies
- Organizations

Value proposition:

- The book version 2.0 with more examples readers sent
- Translated version in French, Spanish
- A Business Model Cube
- A package that includes everything customized for schools, companies, organizations
- One-on-one coaching
- Conferences
- Workshops

Activities:

- Write more stuff
- Answer to questions
- Online marketing
- Attend to book shows and events
- Build a workshop
- Build a business model tool
- Coach people

Team:

- A manager, maybe my sister if she stops being pregnant

Costs:

- Personal assistant
- Online marketing
- Giveaways
- Build the Business Model Cube
- 3d printing

Revenues:

- Conferences/Workshops fees
- Consultancy fees
- Business Model Cube sales

Next step will be to pass each tab in the decision tree of Innovation, seen earlier in Ctrl-T.

And then I'll sort/organize each them at Ctrl-V, where I'll know what sticks or not, and if it does, where.

Ctrl-U: <u>Underline</u>

- Celebrate good times, c'mon!

We too often forget to <u>underline</u> the importance of our efforts, especially in the heat of the action. We are truly our own worst enemy. We better reward him often to avoid his wrath! Most of the time, we expect recognition from others or a gift from heaven, and we forget that others do not care about us—including heaven.

If you don't underline your accomplishments, your successes, and even your failures, who will? No one. Thus, you gradually lose the motivation that is needed every day. Don't be afraid to celebrate. In fact, this is an order.

Starting now, you will underline:

- Each task accomplished.
- Each small victory.
- Each progress.
- Each learning.
- Each failure because it gives you invaluable knowledge, and you can't find anything similar anywhere else.
- Every good piece of work of a colleague, an employee, a friend, a loved one.
- Each moment of courage, tenacity, perseverance.
- Each inspirational story.
- Each challenge.

- Each start.
- Each end.

That leads me to a deep belief that success should mean:

Simple &
Useful
Creation to be
Celebrated at
Every
Single
Step

Remember that you should underline everything, every day. Not once a year! Daily. It will help you stay focused and keep you motivated.

Got it?

My turn

To be honest, I don't underline enough of the things I do nor do I celebrate enough. I am my worst enemy. And a powerful one, trust me.

Too often, I'm expecting external positive feedback or compliments to underline my work. I forget that people care mostly about themselves.

A few years ago I attended a workshop, and there was this guy, I don't remember his name. The only thing I remember from him was his funny face with his beaming smile and what he said that day:

- I used to list all my daily tasks on a sheet and try to do them all, burning myself. Now I limit myself each day to the three most important tasks. After that, I can't do more, I have to take a pause and celebrate. And you know what? A lot more smart things get done this way, and I make more money.

So today, I'll finish this chapter right away and go boating and surfing. See ya!

Your turn

Does it fit with the current Core business?

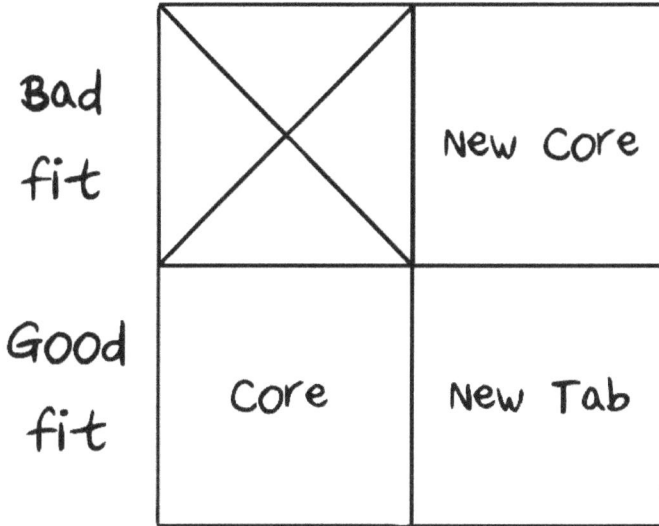

Ctrl-V: Paste

If you want to grow, that means if you want to actually stick to people's day-to-day habits and thereby dominate your current niche market now and in the future, you won't rely only on luck and good timing— you'll need several consecutive good ideas, decisions and new tabs that stick to your business as do thousands of customers.

These new tabs allow you to create an ecosystem around your flag ship product, your core, as did Apple, Coca-Cola, Facebook, Intuit, GE and other large companies that are driven by innovation.

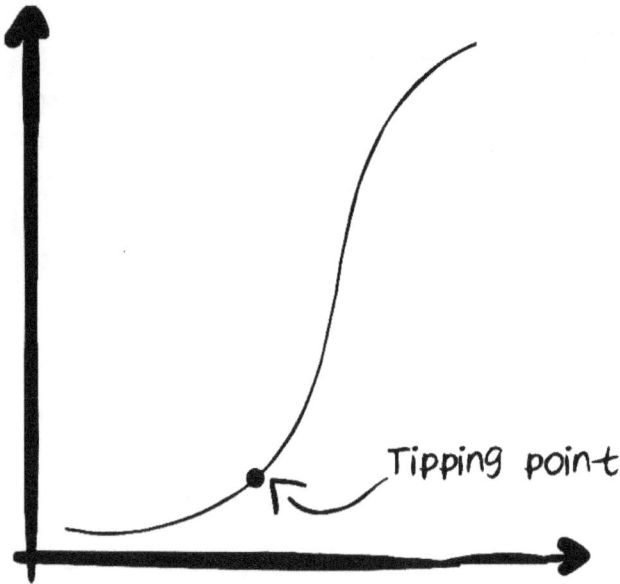

Tipping point

As mentioned previously in Ctrl-T, each time a new tab sticks to customers' needs as well as to your core business, paste it. It could be a new customer segment, a new partner, a new patent, a more efficient process, a new source of revenue, a new cost structure, etc.

Sometimes though, like the case with the companies named above, at some point as you grow, there will be new tabs that stick to customers' needs but that don't stick to the current business because they are incompatible.

This is where you will have to launch a new entity, a new division, a new brand, a new business to meet clients' needs and to not put your current business at stake, avoiding any risk.

Because even if it's the idea of the century, it can (and this is not rare) be incompatible with the current business model or inconsistent with the current customers.

Just like the most beautiful person to you is not the most beautiful to every other people...

As they say, you need chemistry to make things stick.

Ctrl-W: Close tab

- What if the new tab doesn't stick?

Simply close it.

- How do I know if it doesn't stick? How far do I have to persevere before pivoting or closing? How much time, energy, and money?

It depends on how elastic your mental and financial resources are. How much time, energy and money are you willing to invest before you pivot or close the tab? Fix a concrete number of days, of employee hours, of money spent.

A good technique is to ask a few different people their opinion; they should enlighten you (at least they might be better external judges than yourself).

Sometimes, though, closing a tab too quickly is not the best decision, nor is pivoting too fast. As we have seen, people who are successful make quick decisions but rarely change their minds.

- How do I know the perfect time to close a tab?

The best answer is yours. At this point, it's really a matter of intuition. One might sound crazy to put so much effort into what another may see as a stillborn project. But soon he will make him eat his words!

One thing is certain. Don't make the same mistake that

too many people make, which is investing thousands of dollars into something you've built for over six months in your basement without telling anyone, which ends up with zero clients.

Some might say Larry Page and Sergey Brin did this when they built Google. Right.

If you're the next Google, you're the exception to the rule. But let's just say chances are you won't be the next Google.

That brings me back to my premise. Sell first, build after. At worst, if you need something tangible to be able to sell, only build an MVP to minimize your investment and create something creative.

Because we all know the paradox: too much money often kills creativity and creates poor products.

Ctrl-X: Cut

You have a great new tab that fits perfectly with customers' needs, but it turns out that this tab is incompatible with your current business model.

Cut it.

Not in the sense of removing it! Ctrl-X implies that the tab is preserved and will be pasted (Ctrl-V) elsewhere to create or integrate a new business model.

As the new tab can't be inserted into the current business, and you definitely want to take advantage of this new opportunity, create a new core!

- But why would you cut off the tab to create a new entity from it? I thought the goal was to create a company... you did that, right?
- Yes, I did... and I loved it!
- Why don't you continue to grow your company then?!
- Because I am an entrepreneur, not a manager. I like to start, not to manage. I hired a guy for that. My side, I grow my business by undertaking other related and complementary projects. Anyone can manage the known. Only a handful can create the unknown.
- Could you then take a break and do something else other than working?
- Working? I'm having fun!

Your goal was not to create a regular business. Your goal was to create a great company that innovates systematically and dominates its niche market.

Now that it's done, why not use this success as leverage to quickly and violently attack another market next to the one you dominate with this new tab that is super sticky to customers' needs, but can't survive in the environment of the current business model?

This is the opportunity to jump to another level—to serve existing and upcoming customers in a whole new way. Make profits rain by selling a new product to your solid customer base—the customers who have your brand tattooed on their hearts because you solve their picky problems better than anyone else, with a solution that helps them sleep at night—a solution that makes you the #1 player in this niche market.

This is called "cutting the grass under the feet" of competitors.

If you do not believe this, look how small teams succeed as lean as possible and with very little money to create extraordinary things. Just take a look at passionate people crowdfunding their projects on kickstarter.com.

These small teams of two or three people cut out useless things to focus on the core, profits and performance.

They clearly illustrate the recipe of wealth, which I call the 5 P's of Wealth:

1. Purpose
2. Passion
3. People
4. Process
5. Profit

Big companies have become big by applying this process: Amazon, Google, Intuit, Basecamp and so many others who have conquered a niche market and then pulled the rug out from under the feet of competitors from other niche markets by launching an innovative new thing born of the shortcuts sequence Ctrl-T + Ctrl-X + Ctrl-V, which has created a disruptive change and has stuck to people's routine.

My turn

I can't wait to test and validate my new tabs created in Ctrl-T. Until then, can you help me predict what will stick (Ctrl-V) and what won't? Which tab should I close (Ctrl-W)? Which ones should I cut (Ctrl-X) for later, for a new business?

I know it's hard to tell for now, but I like to build some hypotheses to have grounds on something to validate.

What's your opinion on this?

I invite you to do the same exercise for your business.

Their turn — CRTL-S-T-U-V-W-X

Here are the top 15 answers I got in my survey to the questions: "How do you plan to reach THE next level? What's your long-term growth strategy?"

1. I noticed that money is often the reason why a deal cannot process or why a person is not signing up with my company to market their products. So I had the idea of directly financing the sales of my clients, allowing them to process the sale of a house faster.

2. People and their attitude are the innovation policy. Only hire those that fit the mold better than those before. Don't compromise your people unless you want to compromise your future.

3. To reach the next level, I will need to get more partners involved in fields that should be delegated more. In terms of innovating in the presentation & visual communications world, I will definitely keep attending international conferences to share more of that knowledge in French.

4. I love to create new methods of performing the same business activities. I create new websites and allow people to post on them for free. For example: 1) A business card map where businesses showed their locations on a map by their business cards. 2) A social media mashup where we put Facebook like boxes, YouTube videos and tweets from Twitter all on one web page. I also attend as many online events as

possible to learn what is in, but take everyone else's ideas and twist them into our own.

5. Keep the same value, continue to hire the right people the way I do. Build my team and always make room for development. Love my employees. Just continue to do differently. BE DIFFERENT.

6. Make strategic alliances that allow me to make new potential customers networks. Also, develop training using the Internet and Web seminars. Finally, create groups of franchisees that will pay me to teach and use my training materials. All these things should take me to the next level.

7. Our network is invite only. Once we curate 1 000 users on our own, we will let each person invite their top 6 contacts, and they can invite 6 and so on. The exponential network effect will provide solid growth.

8. A Changing Company Culture and asking ourselves the right questions!

9. Keep learning and keep building relationships. Keep trying.

10. Invest in people and projects that align with venture and ecosystem toolbox.

11. Raise money.

12. Webinars.

13. Work harder and smarter.

14. If there is a need to grow larger than 30 people, we will likely spin off a whole new studio rather than increase the size and physical location of the present one. Large studios don't work well. They work, but they churn out employees and mediocre quality. "Innovate or die". That's our policy. If what we're doing is not successful, we kill it fast and move on with a new approach.

15. Next level will mean growing to other platforms and acquiring more users. Long-term growth will include community building and engagement taking on several larger more established marketplaces. Innovation will be our lifeblood; without it, we will never get the disruption we need.

Your turn

Does it fit with the current core business?

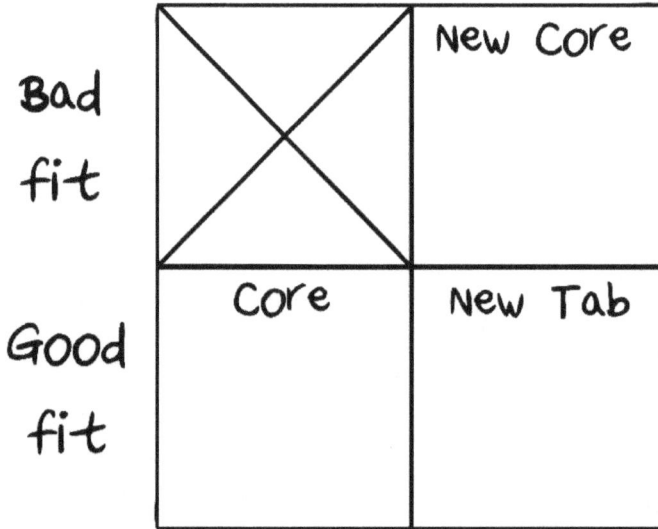

	Current customer (Current value proposition)	Current or New customer (New value proposition)
Bad fit		New Core
Good fit	Core	New Tab

START OVER

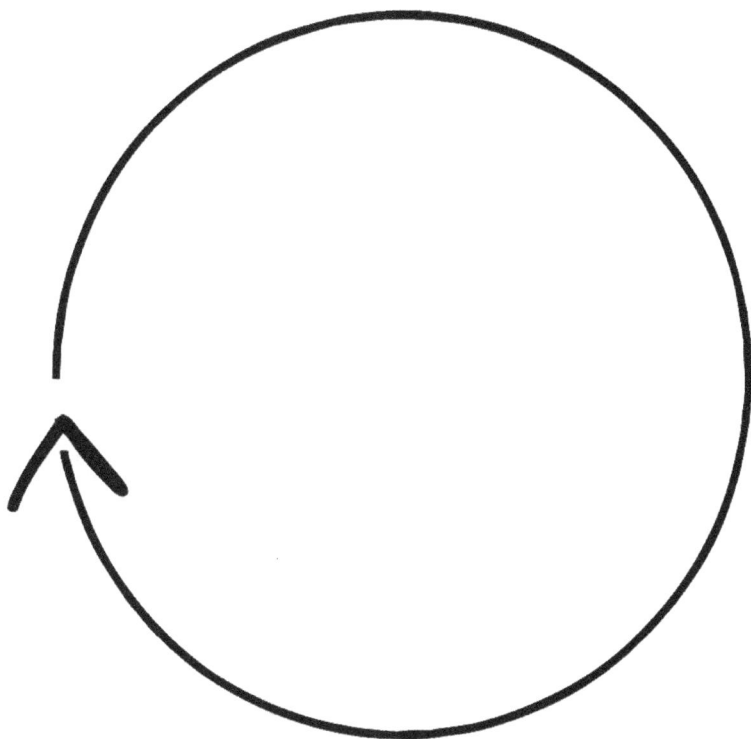

Ctrl-Y: Redo

- But it doesn't work!
- Stop crying. Redo it.

By definition, to redo means doing it again. This could not be clearer!

Some people add to the definition "to redo it, until it works". Brilliant people. But if you really want to innovate and create meaning, you must "redo it, until it works, even if it's freaking long!"

To redo doesn't mean to do the same thing the same way, reproducing the same errors, which would be the exact definition of insanity by Albert Einstein.

Actually, it is to create meaning again and again. To redo what you believe in, to create meaning and succeed in building a business that will make people's lives better.

Some talk about *purpose*. You have built a business based on your personal core. As you grew, you found your own way from the road to the highway. And then you wanted more, much more, because you knew you created a company that carries a deep meaning. Not just for you, but also for the thousands of customers you care about and for the employees that are proud to work with you and excited to wake up every morning and come to work.

You wanted more because it would have been selfish

to stop there. Because you couldn't stop. Because you are on earth for more. That's why you have innovated with new tabs that have improved your current business, and then there was this new tab, which led to this incredible idea; this new product that was not compatible with the current core business. You had to Ctrl-X it.

Now you have to redo again, create a new core, a new brand, a new business inspired by your current business and the actions that led to its creation, revised, redesigned, made differently, transformed. Actually, all of these changes create a bigger impact, a greater change in the lives of people like you.

What's great is that you've already done it once. The second time will be much easier and enjoyable. As proof, compare losing your virginity to the sex you have now.

You get the idea and motivation, but also many things you probably didn't have the first time. The team, hyperlinks, experience, credibility, money and customers. You can list all the saved things that worked: activities, strategies and efforts that are worth redoing.

You can redo them even if you are targeting a new market because most brilliant actions remain shining everywhere; at worst, they go from great to good.

But the important question to ask is: why?

Why have these strategies, activities and efforts resulted in success? After all, we know that luck plays a lot in a result!

Answer this and you will know if you have to redo the same activities, strategies, efforts or team...

More and more, you will be able to accelerate the speed of your decisions, to the point that you will make crucial decisions between two breaths. You create new semi-automatic patterns that work well based on the *If this, then that* method.

If ___*this*___ happens, I need to redo ___*that*___.

In the same way that you stepped up and shortened the time between each iteration with a client, you will do the same with yourself.

From the question ⟶ to the answer.

Then...

From the question → to the answer.

Redoing it again and again will make you stronger. Because what doesn't kill makes you stronger.

You will become stronger, but don't think that you will become the king or the queen of the world. Don't think you can play it easy, sit back and relax! In fact, you can do this if you wish. Many CEOs of large companies have done the same: Blackberry, Nortel, Kodak...

And guess what? They closed their doors! Or almost.

You're not the king of the world, nor are you safe from the two main traps of success:

1. Success stagnation. You can celebrate the success, and it is important to do so—celebrate each small victory as explained in Ctrl-U. But never sit on success. Otherwise, your ass grows, because you eat all your profits, and one day you'll be unable to get up or die from diabetes or from a heart attack.

2. Always redoing what has already been successful, without thinking first. The paradigm of "we've always done it this way, and it worked" is the cancer of any business, any entrepreneur, any singer... How many one-hit wonders do you admire? Zero?

   The way you see your business must be the same.

   Go, redo great things!

My turn

They say it's not about the destination, but about the journey.

I loved writing this book so much that I would redo it anytime. Actually, I will publish a new book, somewhere in 2016. I took a gamble with myself to write one book a year. I also took a gamble with my team to build one MVP a month.

Maybe I'll redo a new edition of this book if I'm bombarded with fascinating stories like yours!

And you: what will you redo?

Your turn

Ctrl-Z: Undo

- A step back? Why go back?

Each action is reversible.

- I feel I will fail... I can't do this!
- So what? Press Ctrl-Z if you miss your shot.

The only way to dance toward achieving a goal for any entrepreneur who doesn't know how to tango, salsa, cha-cha or any *cool and sexy* dance is the sometimes thankless *2 steps forward, one step back* dance.

Taking a step back is also considered taking action because it involves taking a step forward in advance.

Test-Test-Error. Forward-Forward-Backwards. Success-Success-Failure. Cha-Cha-Cha.

Every entrepreneur or enterprise dances to find his way to success.

It may seem impossible or crazy, but every action can be reversed. And now in a split second. Some actions may not be reversible? Really? Be careful not to confuse the action with the result, which is random and depends on several external factors like perception, timing and luck.

So if every action is reversible, why are you afraid of failure?

You can undo in a split second an action based on a strong belief and deep feelings. One moment I LIKE, the next moment I DISLIKE.

This is the era in which we live, which some call the Rewind Reality or the Age of undoing.

What was before a flight of counterfactual fancy is now built right into the interfaces of our daily things that we use to make sense of our shared virtual worlds[7].

You don't follow? Click the BACK button.

This may seem simple and stupid, but it changes a lot of things—if not everything. Starting with the habit that you could quit without consequence. Based on this paradigm shift, you can imagine once unimaginable scenarios and lightning impacts.

In fact, you can *unthink* and enter the wave of *undo*. From all over the world, people are *unthinking*

---

[7] Source: http://www.nytimes.com/2009/09/20/magazine/20FOB-onlanguage-t.html?_r=0

everything that has been thought of by previous generations: old patterns, old patterns: *unmarketing, unconference, unetc.*

It's easy to press Ctrl-Z. Do it!

But do it carefully. Take the time to think twice before taking a step back... in order to then take two steps forward, and not just because you're scared.

Remember that you have to dance your way to the top of your niche market, avoiding the traps of success. The step back shows that you want to innovate and take risks. It works two times, then it crashes one time, works two times, and so on.

You have built your own reality. Ctrl-Z lets you rewind the movie of your destiny and thus reverse the things that you've always believed irreversible.

Un-think old patterns and create disruptive and positive change in people's lives. The same way Toni Braxton did when she un-broke my heart.

My turn

I hate to dance.

I mean, I'm a guy, so I guess that's normal.

I've learned pretty quickly though that I have to know how to dance to make my way to success. You can't imagine how many things I've tried, whether it is marketing techniques or building products. I have to admit the 80/20 rule is true, and maybe too optimistic. I failed a lot more than 80% of the time.

Imagine that the first eight things you build in your life fail. Would you give up or be curious about the next thing you are about to build?

I think the only failure is not to try. Everything else is a success, somehow. Maybe not in the definition of some "Go Big or Fail Big" believers from Texas. But I bet you're not from Texas.

I think that creating a business is a success by itself. But the real deal, in my opinion, is creating a business that employs happy people, starting with you, and solves bold problems to make a better world.

However, if you think you would do this straight from the first try, without any mistake, you're a fool. I'm ready to refund the readers who pretend that, anytime. For the others, you know like me that you have to learn the thankless *two steps forward, one step backwards cha-cha-cha* to success and happiness.

Their turn — CTRL-Y-Z

Here are the top 20 answers I got in my survey to the
questions: "If you had to start over, what would you redo?
What would you undo? What did you learn from this 1st
startup experience?"

1. Every time that I implement a successful strategy,
   I'm making sure that I repeat it over and over again
   while it keeps working for my business. When I first
   joined one of my networking companies, I did not
   see a single sale because I was doing what 99% of
   network marketers do and pushing the business
   opportunity down the prospect's throat. I took a
   step back and I realized that if I focus on the
   PRODUCT instead of the business opportunity, I will
   be more credible for the prospects and it will leave
   them the chance of experiencing the benefits of the
   product. Then they will ask me some questions about
   it. They will be more likely to want to join my
   business opportunity if I demonstrate the benefits
   of the product without even talking about recruiting
   them.

2. Don't wait too long and don't jump too fast. Having
   three years of experience is not enough for you to
   know the market, but having 25 years of experience is
   too much. There is no right time to start a business.
   It took me four tries before it really worked. First,
   not enough experience. Second, not enough contacts.
   Third, I wasn't sure if freelance was what I really
   wanted. And the last time, with everything behind me

and with my experience, I knew what I wanted and how I'd achieve it. My mistakes gave me wisdom.

3. If I had to start over, I would have left my job sooner. Not that I regret it, but the thing I learned was that if you feel like you're being used, then it's probably not a good place to be. And most importantly, make decisions for yourself.

4. It's hard. And not for everyone. The glitz and glam quickly fade for those who are building important things in the world. And for those that aren't, the glitz and glam seem to be the only thing they are building.

5. I would not start out with four shareholders. We are now two, and it's a lot easier.

6. To focus on one place, and work only for me, not for someone else.

7. I don't think I should redo/undo anything, even though I had rough experiences, like any entrepreneur! Those wrong decision or big challenges have made me what I am today, and I could not have learned to deal with them by going from success to success. No regrets from the past, just lessons to move on and improve.

8. I would work out of my house more and not worry about wasting funding on an office until we needed it, since most of our clients asked us to visit them instead. I also would not limit our business to just the U.S. With the Internet, I can get employees from any country and pool their talent more effectively.

9. I would wait before ordering a big volume of products from Italy.

10. I would be more careful in the choice of persons or companies with whom I make alliances. Also, at the human level, we must avoid working with people who are only there to suck your energy. It brings you nothing in return, except trouble.

11. Keep it simpler.

12. I would put more money into ads earlier to gain more momentum early.

13. I would grow my team more selectively and be quicker about trimming the "fat."

14. I would have had more faith in my early ideas, all of them were scalable.

15. To hustle and be persistent with your idea. Talk to customers and build.

16. Become a lawyer.

17. Stick to the original idea and keep testing and tweaking it. Don't change the core of your idea just because you found a really great co-founder at Startup Weekend.

18. Be closer to customers.

19. This is me starting over and this time around I will not compromise on studio values. If you want to work here, you must have a genuine appreciation for

the values of the team. I am not talking about 'rules' or 'interests' but specific virtues such as personal accountability, critical thinking, compassion, passion, etc. We don't hire for academic excellence. We hire first for personal excellence.

20. I'm still building so I have a lot more mistakes to make before starting over. I'm learning that I need to be patient and pragmatic with my time, money and resources.

Your turn

BEGINNING

Ctrl-Enter: Page break

Some would go back to Ctrl-A, because they doubt (and will always doubt) their personal core.

That's not a bad thing if you do the same, but that would mean you didn't put all your heart into the actions that have defined who you are, and not into the idea you have of yourself. But I'm sure that's not the case.

I feel you're now ready to step it up another level. Press Ctrl + Enter and jump right into it. Because opportunities arise into action.

And guess who grabs it? The jumper.

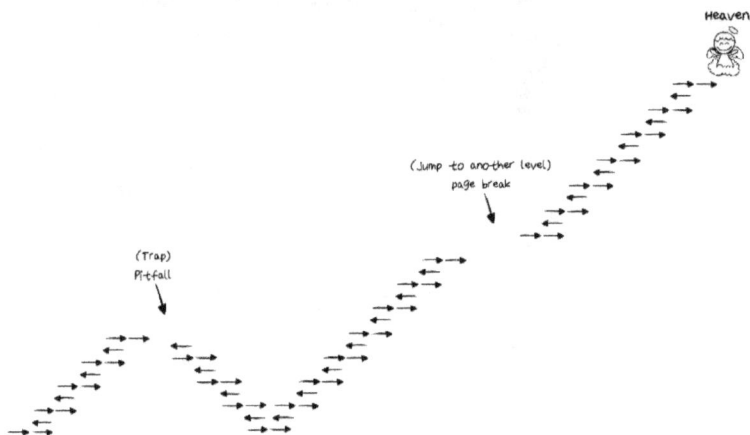

Heaven

(Jump to another level)
page break

(Trap)
Pit-fall

My turn

Like I said at the beginning, this book is an MVP. I invite you to try the 26 shortcuts and write down your story at the end of each chapter. You can also share your story here: http://bit.ly/shortcutstosuccessandhappiness.

For the official marketing launch, I'll post the best stories for each shortcut on www.shortcutstosuccessandhappiness.com, including some of my stories.

I co-founded Code My World with Andu & Bogdan, Demoweb and 20vin20 with Hugo and launched a few products. Quite modest. This is the third book I have written, but the first I have published.

I hope it will help me and my businesses jump to another level where success dances with happiness, in a romance.

See ya there!

Your turn

www.ingramcontent.com/pod-product-compliance
Lightning Source LLC
Chambersburg PA
CBHW021919190326
41519CB00009B/847